I Was Taking Notes

The Book

Dear Reader,

When you are done reading this book, please find someone who may enjoy it and give it to them with the request that when they are done reading it, they pass it on to someone else. It is no good to anyone sitting on a shelf collecting dust. Think of it as Seth Godin *Linchpin* style gift giving.

I Was Taking Notes
The Book

Charlie Mitchell

Cover graphic design by Barbara Mitchell

First Printing: June 2014
Second Printing: July 2015
Third Printing: February 2016
Fourth Printing: April 2016
Fifth Printing: June 2016
Sixth Printing: August 2016
Seventh Printing: November 2016
Eight Printing: March 2017
Ninth Printing: November 2019

Hardcover ISBN 978-0-359-15531-6

Dedication

This book is dedicated *to* my wife and best friend who has shaped me for the better for decades.

This book is *for* my kids, who are shaping up beautifully.

Contents

Acknowledgements

This book could not have been written without many great teachers who intentionally or unintentionally taught me what to do and what not to do in business and in life.

Every manager, every colleague, every client, every competitor, every consultant, and every supplier has taught me something whether they meant to or not. I was constantly looking at people's actions and the results they got. If you ever worked with me, thank you. I was taking notes.

Two deliberate mentors deserve special mention:

1. Jim Talley was my most deliberate business mentor. He had no fear of me surpassing him and was willing to share everything he knew. Whether it was about business writing or hiring an attorney, he was always teaching.

2. John Ault was my first spiritual teacher. His Godly advice and counsel provided me with a solid foundation that pointed me in the right direction with my life and continues to serve me today.

Who will be the next person you learn from? It matters. So choose carefully.

How to Read This Book

This book can be read in any order. As you read, you will see an idea from one chapter appear in another. This is because many things in business and life are connected. A technique designed to fix one problem will also improve other areas.

When you find a topic that you think will help you, put the book aside and research the topic online or get the book cited in the text to read in detail. This book is more of a menu than a meal.

To master everything in this book will take a lifetime of learning and doing. The good news is that you only need to change a few things that you are doing to see improvement in many areas.

Foreword

This book was inspired by Seth Godin's book, *Linchpin*, which explains the value of *doing art* and *giving gifts* in business, and in life. This book is a compilation of things I have learned from others that seem worth passing along. It is my *gift* to the reader.

Don't read every chapter in this book if you don't want to. Feel free to jump around to what interests you.

Half of the contents of this book are things I learned from mentors, by observing others, and by making my own mistakes. The other half are things I learned from some of the greatest books of our time.

Interestingly, these great books often gave me the lens to be able to understand and learn from the events that were happening in my life, usually years later.

So, in the end, I wish to take little credit for these contents, except for the chapters titled *Checklists*, *The Hardest Thing in Business*, and *My Own Inventions*, parts of which, like "Force is rarely the answer," my kids will immediately recognize as classic Dad-isms. I believe they even made a meme for that one.

I want to help people improve their performance – whether they want me to or not, so some of what you read here may sound a little like a rant. I am passionate about improvement. Please take it in the spirit of helpfulness, which is my intent.

Feel free to disagree and feel free to write to me and tell me where I am wrong. Chances are good that you'll end up in my next edition.

Get the most from this book by making your own recipe.

Treat this book like a cookbook. Take ideas from it and make your own recipe for success. It is not a step-by-step guide. That can't work. Collect your own trove of wisdom. Read about how I learned and what I saw and then:

Take your own notes.

Part 1 – Introduction

Eat the meat, spit out the bones.

Chapter 2 Safety Comes from Your Brain

*All the evidence that we have indicates that it is reasonable
to assume in practically every human being, and certainly
in almost every newborn baby, that there is an active will
toward health, an impulse towards growth, or towards the
actualization of human potential.*

~ Abraham Maslow, *Psychologist*

Safety First

Really? This book starts with safety? Really? Why?

In life, if you don't have your health, you can't enjoy life much. In business, if you don't have your health, you can't do business well. Nothing else in business is more important. Nothing.

We used to joke while doing field installation work and say, "Don't get killed. I don't want to do the paperwork." But the truth is I don't want to have to call your family and tell them you got hurt just so we could make an extra dollar in profit.

Use Your Brain

When planning any action, just take a moment to think about the short-term future and try to predict what might happen as a result of what you are planning to do.

Using your brain to ask, "What if?" is the best safety practice there is. It's cheap and everyone can have it in their toolkit.

- What will happen to the far end of this board if I step on this end?
- What will happen if I tie this rope to the bumper of a parked truck?
- If I leave these things here, will they be safe while I am gone?
- If this blade suddenly cuts through, what will happen?
- What will happen if I lean this next to this door?
- What might happen if I ignore the gauge and keep on driving?

Look Out for Each Other

Just like they teach you in Kindergarten.

Years ago, I had a crew of under-trained, under-equipped laborers working for a subcontractor on a project of mine on the Texas-Mexico border. One man was chipping concrete with a hammer and chisel. He had no eye protection, so I asked him:

"Do you have kids?

"Yes. Two boys and a girl."

"Do you want to see them as they grow up?"

(Puzzled look) "Yes."

I handed him my safety glasses. "Then wear these. You can keep them."

I did this on several occasions on that job site. After that, whenever they saw me, the guys would smile at me and point at their safety glasses. I made eye safety a personal benefit to them, not a rule from the boss. I often wondered how they told the story at home that night.

> Isn't it easiest to see when someone else is in peril?
> Help them to see the possible result before it's too late.

Safe Coding

Interestingly, one of the tenants of the new wave of agile software development is the notion that the best software is created in a safe environment. Only when the creative mind is not distracted by the politics of a competitive or socially threatening environment can the very best work be done. Emotional safety has a business benefit.

Gender-specific references are not intended to limit the statement to gender-specific results. Unless noted otherwise, *he* can readily be substituted for *she*, and vice versa.

Ten Commandments for the Service Technician

1. Beware the Lightning that Lurketh in the Undischarged Capacitor, lest it Smite Thee and cause Thee to Bounce upon Thy buttocks in a most Un-technician-like Manner.

2. Causeth the Switch that Supplieth large quantities of Voltage to be Opened and Thusly Tagged, so that Thy Days may be Long.

3. Prove to Thyself that all Circuits that Radiateth, and Upon Which Thou Workest, are Grounded, and have their Power Reduced or Removed, lest they Lift Thee to Thy Radio Frequency Potential and causeth Thee to Act like a Radiator also.

4. Tarry not amongst those Fools that engage in Intentional Shock; for Verily they are surely Non-Believers and are not Long for this World.

5. Take care that Thou Useth the Proper Method when Thou takest Measurements of High Voltage, lest thee Incinerate both Thyself and Thy Meter. While Thee hath no Inventory Number and can therefore be Easily Replaced, Thy Meter doth have an Inventory Number and Replacement bringeth much Woe unto the Purchasing Officer.

6. Tamperest not with Interlocks and Safety Switches, for this Incurreth the Wrath of Thy Supervisor and Bringeth the Fullness of the Fury of the Safety Inspector down upon Thy meager Head.

7. Workest not on Fully-Energized Equipment, for if Thou so Dost, Thy Funeral Home shall surely Console Thy Widow.

8. Workest not on Equipment alone, for Electrical Cooking is a slothful process and Thou might Sizzle in Thy own Fat for Hours upon the Circuit before Thy Maker sees fit to end Thy Misery.

9. Triflest not with Radioactive Tubes and Substances, lest Thou Commence to Glow in the Dark like the Firefly, and Thy Spouse have no Further use for Thee except Thy Wages.

10. Thou must Forceth Thyself to Document all Modifications made by Thee upon Equipment, lest Thy Successor tear His Hair out and go slowly Mad in His attempt to Decide what manner of Creature hath made a Nest in the Wiring of such Equipment.

Chapter 3 You Must Constantly Train

*Reading is for the improvement of the understanding. The
improvement of the understanding is for two ends; first, for
our own increase of knowledge; secondly, to enable us to
deliver and make out that knowledge to others.*

~ John Locke, *1689*

Need for Training

Jim Collins tells the story of a company executive discussing the cost
of providing training to their considerable number of employees.

The executive asks, "What if we train them and they all leave?"

To which the consultant responds, "What if you don't train them and
they all stay?"

I Already Have a College Degree

If you are thinking, "Well, I already know everything I need to know
to do my job," you are a sitting duck.

I owe a debt of gratitude to Chuck Andrews for teaching me two things.
He was a seasoned field application engineer at B&K Instruments when
I was a novice customer support engineer. He said, "If you don't seek
continuous education, your four year college degree is going to be thirty
years out of date at the end of your career. Don't depend on anyone else
to tell you what training you need. Take charge."

Picture yourself changing jobs at 55 or 60 years of age. Are you current
in your skill and knowledge? In theory, you should be extremely valuable at that point if you have continuously invested in yourself.

Do you think any of your competitors are sitting still? I don't mean
your company's competitors, I mean the people who want the job you
want.

I Have Not Been Selected for Training

I have met many people who say that they have not learned this or that
because they have not been sent to get training. There are two things
wrong with this statement. First, you should not wait for anyone else to

decide what training you should have. Second, if you have access to the Internet, you can teach yourself a lot for free.

Management consultant, Malcolm Pancoast, taught that *Be, Do, Have* was the right sequence for success. Don't worry about the trappings of formal education for something, just start *Being*, and then *Doing* that thing, and the rest will follow. *See page 83.*

I Don't Need No Book Learning

I had an ignorant colleague, who was resistant to change in general, once argue with me about learning new ways to do business from books like Jim Collin's, *Good to Great,* and Pat Lencioni's, *The Five Dysfunctions of a Team*. He said that we had no way of knowing if the authors of management books knew what they were talking about.

"We probably know more than they do." he said.

Really? How does he think publishing works?

Does he think these guys write a bunch of nonsense and then trick hundred year old business publishing companies and industry reviewers? Does it become a best seller and sell over four million copies because it is no good? Sorry, that dog won't hunt. If you think you know so much about your field that you cannot learn from experts who research the things that make businesses succeed, you are sadly mistaken.

Two Kinds of Experience

There are two approaches to gaining work experience. One is where you do the same thing for 30 years. The other is where you constantly experiment and try different methods and do different jobs and keep what works and constantly weed your garden of techniques and behaviors that no longer serve you. In other words, *change your methods.*

Too often people do the same thing over and over so that at the end of a twenty five year career at a company, they really only have a year's experience repeated over and over.

Change Your Methods

In conventional thinking about projects, many will say of *good, fast, and cheap* that you must pick only two. I say you can have all three *if you are willing to change your methods*.

Change your methods, first by always learning, and second, by doing the work of applying what you learn.

This second part of applying what you have learned is the hard work that many are not willing to do. When I did the toll system project for the Golden Gate Bridge, I knew there was no chance that our current methods could meet the customer's schedule, but agile software development methods held the promise of speeding delivery. We created a new, small team and put them in a new, remote office and ran a skunkworks style operation with Scrum and Test Driven Development and it was *good, fast, and cheap.*

If you are willing to learn new things and put them into practice, you will have an advantage in business and in life. If you do it once, the effect will be temporary. If you make a lifelong practice of *changing your methods*, you will have a constant advantage over your peers and competitors.

◆ ◆ ◆ ◆ ◆

The Second Thing

The second thing that Chuck Andrews taught me was the look of a dress shirt with the sleeves rolled up. When I saw him roll up his sleeves to work on an equipment set-up, it just broadcast to the room that here was a sharply dressed man who was serious about getting the job done. His look accurately reflected his attitude and even a passer-by could see it.

Chapter 4 Nothing New Under the Sun

*That which has been is that which will be, and that which
has been done is that which will be done.*

So there is nothing new under the sun.

~ Ecclesiastes 1:9, *NASB*

That's Not New!

Much of the value of modern management teaching is how to organize
our thinking about what we already know. I call this the *Ecclesiastes
Knowledge Theory* – "There is nothing new under the sun."

So the fundamental truths that we look at in a management system are
rarely completely new, undiscovered, stunning revelations, but rather
established truths organized in a way that we better understand.

New Handles

When I write about how there is nothing new under the sun, it is a way
of saying that most modern business management books are simply explaining common sense concepts in new ways that allow us to wield
that information more deftly and to be effective with it. Often this is by
assembling it in new patterns or giving us frameworks that give us a
handle to latch onto and a template for applying it.

Exceptional Luck

As an exception to this, I am always pleased to cite Jim Collins as an
author who has done substantial, original research, together with his
highly respected management research team in Boulder Colorado, and
produced new information. This was true of the work that created *Good
to Great,* and equally true of *Great by Choice*, where Jim Collins studied the impact of luck on businesses. Simply put, it is not a great stroke
of luck that makes a business great over time. It is how companies react
to luck, good and bad, that determines whether or not they will succeed.
Collin's research shows that all businesses come into both good and
bad luck and it is how they respond to luck that makes the difference.
No one had ever studied this scientifically before.

So Then, What is New Learning?

Just because you are aware of something does not mean you understand it well.

Aware ≠ Grok

Grok is an old geek-speak term. It comes from Robert Heinlein's 1961 science fiction classic, *Stranger in a Strange Land*. It means to completely understand the nature of something. It literally means *to drink* an idea or concept. This concept reappeared in the hit movie Avatar, with the expression "I see you."

So, when we read a popular management book, we might not say, "Well! Here is a concept that is completely new to me!" However, we may still gain new, greater understanding because of the way it is exposed, clarified, and connected to other ideas.

The new things we learn are:

- Glimpses into the mirror looking at our own behavior
- Understanding something that was always there
- Connecting two previously separate thoughts or concepts
- Categorizing thoughts into a new framework or taxonomy

The end result is that we can locate, access, retrieve, and use this information more effectively. This is significant; because the only information that counts is the information you can access and apply quickly.

I have met countless people who have read, *The Seven Habits of Highly Effective People* and *The One Minute Manager,* who cannot remember anything from them. They have gained no knowledge.

Knowledge is not power, the application of knowledge is power.

Part 2 – Performance

Decide to improve your performance step-by-step for
the rest of your life.

Chapter 5 Seven Habits

Do you believe that in the next half-hour you could learn something that will profoundly change your life for the better? Do you believe that all big, positive change comes with advance notice?

Those were two questions asked to the 2011 class of interns at Clever Devices, Ltd. right before I taught about the *Seven Habits*. They all answered that *yes*, they believed their lives could change right then, without notice.

I wonder what happens when you ask those questions to a bunch of 50 year-olds.

Most Recommended

Of all of the things I have learned and taught over the years, Stephen Covey's, *The 7 Habits of Highly Effective People*, is the book I most readily recommend to individuals seeking to improve their lives.

The 7 Habits moves us through the following stages:

1. **Dependence**: the paradigm under which we are born, relying upon others to take care of us.
2. **Independence**: the paradigm under which we can make our own decisions and take care of ourselves.
3. **Interdependence**: the paradigm under which we cooperate with others to achieve something that cannot be achieved independently.

Personal Mission Statement

Stephen Covey recommends that we live according to principle-based, personal mission statements. This feeds right into *Habit #2*. Here are my practical steps to use Covey's idea and get started on yours:

Step 1 – Make a list of one-word items that are important to you (kids, education, God, health, etc.).
Step 2 – Put them in order of importance.
Step 3 – Identify one activity that if you did it superbly well and consistently would produce marvelous results in your personal or family life.

Step 4 – Identify one activity that if you did it superbly well and consistently would produce marvelous results in your work or professional life.

The answers to steps 3 and 4 should help you obtain the other things you have identified in step 1. Focus on them.

Alternative Approach - Write your own eulogy.

Who would want to come to your funeral? Who matters to you? To whom do you matter? In creating a principle based mission statement, you should find that you are creating a new paradigm – principles and relationships, not things and schedules. It's a start. Here's mine:

> *To honor God by being a loving, kind, giving, effective, and responsible husband, father, employee, community, and church member. This means to nurture my wife, prepare my kids for life, deliver value far in excess of my cost to my company, improve my community by my actions, and fulfill my calling in the kingdom of God.*

Summary of *The 7 Habits of Highly Effective People*

I hope the following summary encourages you to read Stephen Covey's book, *The 7 Habits of Highly Effective People,* for yourself.

Habit 1: Be Proactive

Change starts from within, and highly effective people make the decision to improve their lives through the things that they can influence rather than by simply reacting to external forces.

Take initiative in life by realizing that your decisions (and how they align with life's principles) are the primary determining factor for effectiveness in your life. Take responsibility for your choices and the subsequent consequences that follow.

To be proactive means to change your mind; to think about your thinking.*

	URGENT	NOT URGENT
IMPORTANT	Quadrant 1 **Necessity** -------------- Response: **Manage** -------------- *Examples*: - Crises - Deadline driven activities - Medical emergencies - Other *true* emergencies - Pressing problems - Last minute preparations	Quadrant 2 **Hyperproductivity** -------------- Response: **Focus** -------------- *Examples*: - Preparation and planning - Values clarification - Empowerment - Relationship building - True recreation
NOT IMPORTANT	Quadrant 3 **Low Value** -------------- Response: **Explain then Avoid** -------------- *Examples:* - Meeting other people's priorities and expectations - Frequent interruptions - Most emails, some calls - Urgency pretending to be importance	Quadrant 4 **Distraction** -------------- Response: **Avoid** -------------- *Examples:* - Escapist activities - Mindless TV - Busywork - Junk mail - Some emails, phone calls

* This is how it all started for me. Professor Ryerson, who taught marketing at Clarkson, shared the *Eisenhower Method's* four quadrants of urgency and importance, which Stephen R. Covey popularized in *The 7 Habits of Highly Effective People*. This prompted me, for the first time, to think about the process of thinking about how I think. I did not even know what had happened at the time.

Habit 2: Begin with the End in Mind

Develop a principle-centered personal mission statement. Extend the mission statement into long-term goals based on personal principles.

Self-discover and clarify your deeply important character values and life goals. Envision the ideal characteristics for each of your various roles and relationships in life.

According to Covey, Merrill, and Merrill, (*First Things First*; 1994, p. 113), an empowering mission statement:

1. Represents the deepest and best within you. It comes out of a solid connection with your deep inner life.

2. Is the fulfillment of your own unique gifts. It's the expression of your unique capacity to contribute.
3. Is transcendent. It's based on principles of contribution and purpose higher than self.
4. Addresses and integrates all four fundamental human needs and capacities. It includes fulfillment in physical, social, mental, and spiritual dimensions. ["To live, to love, to learn, to leave a legacy."]
5. Is based on principles that produce quality-of-life results.
6. Deals with both vision and principle-based values. An empowering mission statement deals with both character and competence; what you want to be and what you want to do in your life.
7. Deals with all the significant roles in your life. It represents a lifetime balance of personal, family, work, community – whatever roles you feel are yours to fill.
8. Is written to inspire you – not to impress anyone else. It communicates to you and inspires you on the most essential level.

Habit 3: Put First Things First

Spend time doing what fits into your personal mission, observing the proper balance between production and building production capacity. Identify the key roles that you take on in life, and make time for each of them. Plan, prioritize, and execute your week's tasks based on importance rather than urgency, evaluating whether your efforts exemplify your desired character values, propel you toward goals, and enrich the roles and relationships that were elaborated in *Habit 2*.

Habit 4: Think Win/Win

Seek agreements and relationships that are mutually beneficial. In cases where a *win/win* deal cannot be achieved, accept the fact that agreeing to make *no deal* may be the best alternative. In developing an organizational culture, be sure to reward *win/win* behavior among employees and avoid inadvertently rewarding *win/lose* behavior.

Genuinely strive for mutually beneficial solutions or agreements in your relationships. Value and respect people by understanding a *win* for all is ultimately a better long-term resolution than if only one person in the situation has his way.

Habit 5: Seek First to Understand, Then to Be Understood

First seek to understand the other person, and only then try to be understood. Stephen Covey presents this habit as the most important principle of interpersonal relations. Effective listening is not simply echoing what the other person has said through the lens of one's own experience. Rather, it is putting oneself in the perspective of the other person, listening empathically for both feeling and meaning.

Use empathetic listening to be genuinely influenced by a person, which compels them to reciprocate the listening and have an open mind to being influenced by you. This creates an atmosphere of caring, respect, and positive problem solving.

Habit 6: Synergize

Through trustful communication, find ways to leverage individual differences to create a whole that is greater than the sum of the parts. Through mutual trust and understanding, one often can solve conflicts and find a better solution than would have been obtained through either person's own solution.

Combine the strengths of people through positive teamwork, so as to achieve goals no one person could have alone. Get the best performance out of a group of people by encouraging meaningful contribution, and modeling inspirational and supportive leadership.

Habit 7: Sharpen the Saw

Take time out from production to build production capacity through personal renewal of the physical, mental, social/emotional, and spiritual dimensions. Maintain a balance among these dimensions.

Balance and renew your resources, energy, and health to create a sustainable, long-term, effective lifestyle.

Stephen Covey says the only way to really understand these 7 *Habits* is to teach them to others.

Chapter 6 Five Dysfunctions

*Not finance. Not strategy. Not technology. It is teamwork
that remains the ultimate competitive advantage,
both because it is so powerful and so rare.*

~ Patrick Lencioni, *The Five Dysfunctions of a Team*

About the Management Fable

The Five Dysfunctions of a Team is the fictional story of a new CEO
brought in to fix the lack of teamwork at a tech start-up company that
has all the right pieces, but can't seem to take advantage of their situation because they can't function correctly.

A Friendly Word of Warning

I don't recommend this book lightly. While I am always happy to recommend Stephen Covey's, *The Seven Habits of Highly Effective
People,* to any individual, and I am happy to recommend Jim Collins's,
Good to Great, or *Great by Choice*, to any company, this book by Patrick Lencioni, is dangerous material.

Once you start poking around at how your management team functions
by using the tools that Patrick Lencioni suggests, there will be nowhere
for incompetent or selfish team members to hide. This process shines a
light on every bad behavior.

If you corner a dysfunctional manager in this way, they will react de-
fensively, attacking both you and the change process itself. Chances are
good that if you complete the healing process, not everyone who is
there at the beginning will still be there at the end.

Be careful not to blow up your company with dangerous truth.
Just because something is true does not mean you should say it.

Five Functions

Patrick Lencioni describes five functions that a team needs to perform well that can completely change their effectiveness.

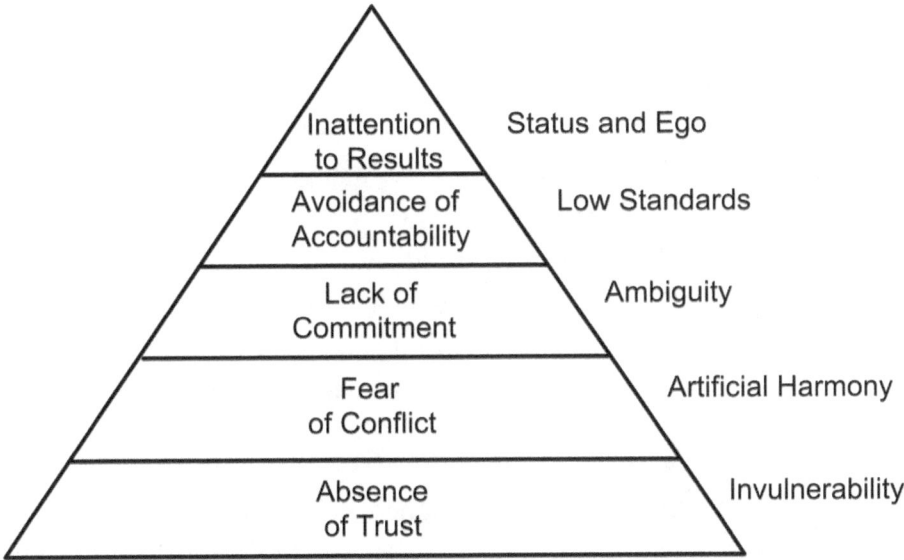

Amazing results can be obtained by getting people to:

1. Speak what they really believe

2. Engage in productive conflict and honest debate

3. Clarify ambiguity, make clear decisions, and communicate the decisions outside the team

4. Hold one another responsible to follow through

5. Put group goals ahead of individual goals

Lencioni explains that politics is when people choose their words and actions based on how they want others to react rather than based on what they know is true.

When team members trust each other, they can speak the truth. In this context, *trust* is not used in the "touchy-feely" sense. Instead, it means feeling safe enough around the team to say what you truly believe and not be thinking about what you should say for politics.

Chapter 7 Speed of Trust

Trust always affects two outcomes—speed and cost.

~ Stephen M. R. Covey, *The Speed of Trust*

Two Outcomes

Trust always affects two outcomes—speed and cost. When trust goes down, speed will also go down and costs will go up. When trust is up, speed goes up and costs go down.

Low Trust = Low Speed and Higher Cost
(resulting in a *trust tax*)

High Trust = High Speed and Low Cost
(resulting in a *trust dividend*)

Five Waves of Trust

In his book, *The Speed of Trust*, Stephen M. R. Covey promotes the concept of five waves of trust. The five waves of trust are derived from the *ripple effect* metaphor that graphically illustrates the interdependent nature of trust and how it flows from the inside out.

Trust Wave 1: Self Trust

This is having credibility by having confidence in ourselves and having the ability to inspire trust in others. This goes beyond *ethics* and explains why personal credibility is the foundation of all trust. Covey describes the *4 Cores of Credibility*, which are vital to credibility and trust, and how we can improve them in a way that increases trust on every level from the inside out.

- Core 1: Integrity (Character)

- Core 2: Intent (Character)

- Core 3: Capabilities (Competence)

- Core 4: Results (Competence)

Trust Wave 2: Relationship Trust

This is having a consistent behavior in order to establish and increase the *trust accounts* we have with others.

Here, Covey gives us the 13 behaviors that significantly enhance our ability to establish trust in all relationships. They are powerful because they are based on principles that govern trusting relationships. They grow out of the 4 Cores. They are actionable, and they are universal.

1. Talk straight
2. Demonstrate respect
3. Create transparency
4. Right wrongs
5. Show loyalty
6. Deliver results
7. Get better
8. Confront reality
9. Clarify expectations
10. Practice accountability
11. Listen first
12. Keep commitments
13. Extend trust

Trust Wave 3: Organizational Trust

By having alignment, leaders can generate trust with all kinds of organizations by creating structures, systems, and symbols of organizational trust. Covey lists seven symbols that represent a low-trust organization (taxes) and seven symbols that represent a high-trust organization (dividends).

The 7 Low-Trust Organizational Taxes™

Redundancy: Redundancy is unnecessary duplication. A costly redundancy tax is often paid in excessive organizational hierarchy, layers of management, and overlapping structures designed to ensure control.

Bureaucracy: Bureaucracy includes complex and cumbersome rules, regulations, policies, procedures, and processes. One estimate put the cost of complying with federal rules and regulations at $1.1 trillion, more than 10 percent of the GDP in the US alone.

Politics: Office politics divide a culture against itself. The result is wasted time, talent, energy, and money. In addition, they poison company cultures, derail strategies and sabotage initiatives, relationships and careers.

Disengagement: Disengagement occurs when people put in enough effort to avoid getting fired but don't contribute their talent, creativity, energy or passion. Gallup's research puts a price tag of $250 - $300 billion a year on the cost of disengagement.

Turnover: Employee turnover represents a huge cost, and in low-trust companies, turnover exceeds the industry standard – particularly of the people you least want to lose. Good performers like to be trusted and they like to work in high-trust environments.

Churn: Churn is the turnover of stakeholders other than employees. When trust inside an organization is low, it gets perpetuated in interactions in the marketplace, causing great turnover among customers, suppliers, distributors, and investors. Studies indicate the cost of acquiring a new customer versus keeping an existing one is as much as 500 percent.

Fraud: Fraud is flat out dishonesty, sabotage, obstruction, deception, and disruption – and the cost is enormous. One study estimated that the average U.S. company loses six percent of its annual revenue to some sort of fraudulent activity.

The 7 High-Trust Organizational Dividends™

Increased value: Watson Wyatt shows high-trust organizations outperform low-trust organizations in total return to shareholders by 286 percent.

Accelerated growth: Research clearly shows customers buy more, buy more often, refer more, and stay longer with companies they trust. And, these companies actually outperform with less cost.

Enhanced innovation: High creativity and sustained innovation thrive in a culture of high trust. The benefits of innovation are clear – opportunity, revenue growth, and market share.

Improved collaboration: High-trust environments foster the collaboration and teamwork required for success in the new global economy.

Without trust, collaboration is mere coordination, or at best, cooperation.

Stronger partnering: A Warwick Business School study shows that partnering relationships that are based on trust experience a dividend of up to 40 percent of the contract.

Better execution: Franklin Covey's execution quotient tool (xQ) has consistently shown a strong correlation between higher levels of organizational execution and higher levels of trust. In a 2006 study of grocery stores, top executing locations had significantly higher trust levels than lower executing locations in every dimension measured.

Heightened loyalty: High-trust companies elicit far greater loyalty from their primary stakeholders than low-trust companies. Employees, customers, suppliers, distributors, and investors stay longer.

Trust Wave 4: Market Trust

Establish and maintain a reputation with business partners outside the organization, building trust and loyalty.

Reputation = Brand = Trust in the Marketplace

Build your brand (your reputation), and thereby your trust in the marketplace, by applying the 4 Cores and the 13 Behaviors.

Trust Wave 5: Societal Trust

Creating value for others and society at large by the contribution that is made or, *by giving back.*

The overriding principle of societal trust is contribution. The principle of contribution is the intent to create value instead of to destroy it, to give back instead of to take, and to be a responsible global citizen.

Chapter 8 Change

Nothing is so painful to the human mind as a great and sudden change.

~ Mary Shelley, *Frankenstein (1818)*

In their book, *Switch*, Chip and Dan Heath explored the psychology of change and created practical guidelines on how to create successful changes by addressing three different parts of the change problem. Many people's approach to change is to *just wish for it and hope it comes along by magic.*

The Heaths teach that change is skilled work that can be best achieved by attending to all three parts of the problem of human change. They use the analogy of a rider, an elephant, and a path. To have the best chance of success, you must work on all three, or at least have all three working in your favor.

Part 1 – Rational

Direct the Rider (the intellectual part of the mind):

- Find the existing good examples – *Find the "Bright Spots" – existing examples of success that model what you want*

- Define the desired actions and methods – *Script the Critical Moves*

- Clearly identify the goals and objectives – *Point to the Destination*

Part 2 – Emotional

Motivate the Elephant (the feeling part of the mind):

- Create an emotional motivation – *Find the Feeling*

- Define small, manageable increments of improvement – *Shrink the Change*

- Build capacity for change and new things – *Grow Your People*

Part 3 – Situational

Shape the Path (the circumstances you live and work in):

- Change conditions so they favor the change – *Tweak the Environment*
- Start small behaviors that promote the change – *Build Habits*
- Align people to support change – *Rally the Herd*

◆　◆　◆　◆　◆

Culture Change

Business cartoonist, Hugh McLeod, says that real culture change starts with real emotional change. On some level, this has to be a cathartic experience, maybe not for the entire company, but certainly for a few key leaders. "Nothing happens until somebody feels something," is how he describes it.

I agree. I think you are wasting your time until the senior leadership *get it,* and are so convinced of the need for change that they won't let go of it.

◆　◆　◆　◆　◆

I was thinking about some colleagues whose business is in trouble and I realized that even all of Solomon's wisdom won't help people who are not truly interested in change. It is often said:

People don't mind change, they mind being changed.

~ Unknown

Bill McAneny wrote in his blog *(Feb 4, 2008)*:

> You know how when we go into a store and we just love buying things, but when the salesperson comes over to speak to us we go rigid and walk out? That's because we love buying but we can't stand being sold to. This principle is the same with change, we love it if it's something we do, but hate it when it is done to us.

> I had the senior team from a client gathered to look at the future shape of their business. They weren't too pleased. Their collective view was that they were masters of change, they lived out change every day and they needed no one to help them 'manage change'. I couldn't get them to even admit that they themselves might have to change, so I gave each of them an envelope with their name on it. They were really suspicious and opened them carefully and inside were their termination notices.

> Well, that livened the party up! They got really irate, and then a few of the more astute ones noticed that it was dated two years hence. So I said to go away and look back on that session with the psy-chologist and tell me why you were made redundant, what didn't you do which you should have, what did you do which you should not have.

> While they were out of the room, I re-arranged the tables, which were in a half circle, to be more 'cabaret' style, just because that's how I prefer it, no ulterior motive. Well, when the team came back they were totally disoriented. Of the 17 executives from one of the world's biggest companies, none knew where to sit, there was total confusion, and they all looked to me for the lead.

And the moral of this tale? We like change when it is something we do, but not when it is something which is done to us.

♦ ♦ ♦ ♦ ♦

When people are ready to, they change. They never do it before then, and sometimes they die before they get around to it. You can't make them change if they don't want to, just like when they do want to, you can't stop them.

~ Andy Warhol

♦ ♦ ♦ ♦ ♦

Change means different things to different people. Everyone will tell you they change. No one thinks they are stagnant. So what is the standard?

I propose that *if you are not willing to change as fast as the state of the art, you are not really willing to change* in a meaningful way.

Throughout history people have resisted change, saying things like:

- I am not willing to use a stick club
- I am not willing to use a flint knife
- I am not willing to use fire
- I am not willing to use a wheel
- I am not willing to use a printing press
- I am not willing to use a clock
- I am not willing to use a steam engine
- I am not willing to use an automobile
- I am not willing to use electricity
- I am not willing to use a telegraph
- I am not willing to use a telephone
- I am not willing to use a typewriter
- I am not willing to use a copier
- I am not willing to use a facsimile machine
- I am not willing to use a personal computer
- I am not willing to use a cell phone
- I am not willing to use the Internet
- I am not willing to use Napster/Myspace (social media)
- I am not willing to use online shopping
- I am not willing to use SMS texting
- I am not willing to use telecommuting
- I am not willing to use a GPS
- I am not willing to use an iPod
- I am not willing to use a Smartphone
- I am not willing to use Facebook/Twitter (social media)
- I am not willing to use cloud computing
- I am not willing to use Snapchat/Instagram (social media)
- I am not willing to use a tablet computer
- I am not willing to use a wrist computer
- I am not willing to use a self-driving car
- I am not willing to use bionic limbs
- I am not willing to use Google Glass/Augmented Reality
- I am not willing to use a computer chip brain implant
- I am not willing to teleport
- I am not willing to use a virtual assistant

- I am not willing to use the IBM Watson cognitive server
- I am not willing to travel off-world
- I am not willing to grow new organs
- I am not willing to use artificial intelligence
- I am not willing to use an android personal assistant
- I am not willing to use an Nth dimensional computer
- I am not willing to use a meshed consciousness (yet more social media)

Where are you on the continuum?

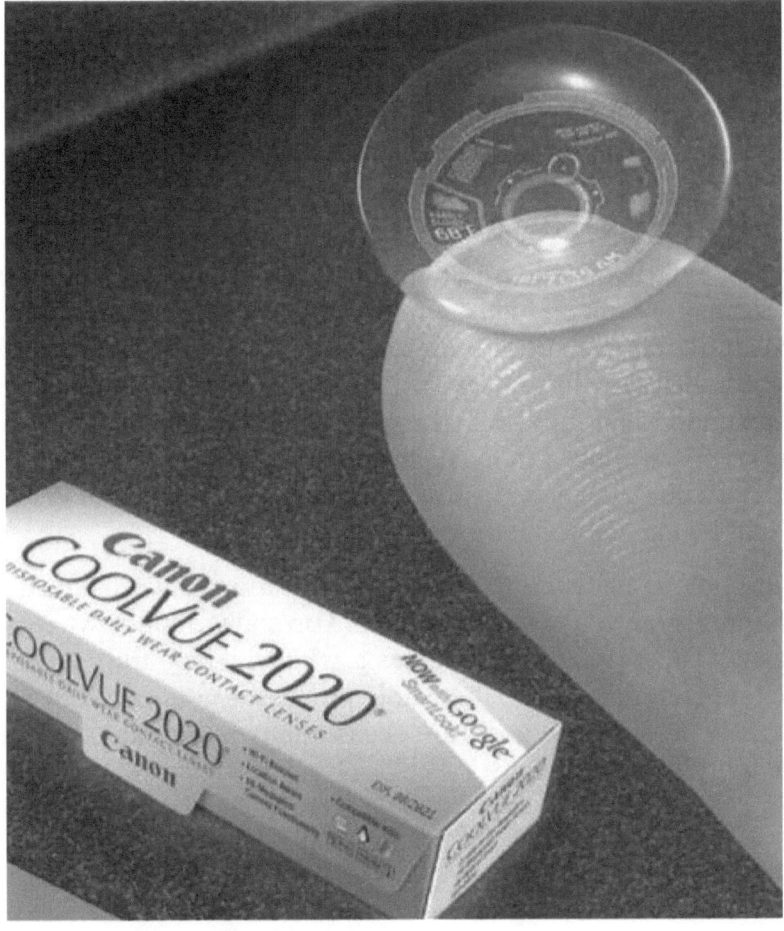

Chapter 9 One Minute Management

Levy continued, "In most organizations, the managers spend their time catching people doing what?" he asked the young man.

The young man smiled and answered knowingly, "Doing something wrong."

"Right!" said Levy, "Here we put the accent on the positive. We catch people doing something right!"

~ Ken Blanchard, *The One Minute Manager*

Quick Read

Get the classic 106 page book, *The One Minute Manager*, by Ken Blanchard. It can easily be read in a single sitting. It addresses the most prevalent work problem: communication failures. Specifically, it addresses communicating assignments, successes, and failures.

One Minute Goal Setting

Have you ever had a miscommunication about an assignment? Sure, everyone has. The book focuses on the role of the manager, but there is responsibility on the part of both parties to get clarity. I like to tell my employees that they have every right to insist on clear instruction that they can understand fully. Whether your manager uses one minute goal setting or not, you need to make sure that you get the information you need. If you don't get good instructions, chances are you, not your manager, will be blamed for getting it wrong.

Setting *One Minute Goals* requires a conversation between the manager and the employee where goals are agreed on and written down in a brief statement. This setting process takes a *minute*, which truly means it is a quick meeting. However, the whole process is not limited to just the initial sixty seconds; the goals are occasionally reviewed to ensure that productivity is occurring.

The focus of the *One-Minute Goal Setting* approach is to assume that there is a problem to be solved and that you should describe it in behavioral terms, which means *describing the difference* between what is now happening and what you want to happen. Ken Blanchard wrote:

> *"I mean, the manager explained to me, that I do not want to hear about only attitudes or feelings. Tell me what is happening in observable, measurable terms."*

> *"If you can't tell me what you'd like to be happening,"* he said, *"you don't have a problem yet; you're just complaining. A problem only exists if there is a difference between what is* <u>actually</u> *happening and what you* <u>desire</u> *to be happening."*

Once we have a behavioral description of what is currently happening, we can describe what we want to have happen. Then we will be able to test any proposed solution by imagining the expected outcome and comparing it with the desired behavior. If the expected outcome does not match the needed outcome, you don't have a good solution.

The main purpose of one minute goal setting is to confirm that responsibilities of each assignment are well understood, but if we also described these:

- What – results;
- Why – benefit to be obtained;
- How – actions, steps, path;
- When – deadline;
- How much – expected costs;
- Other resources – with whom, with what; and,

then we can periodically check in and verify that the work is going as agreed upon.

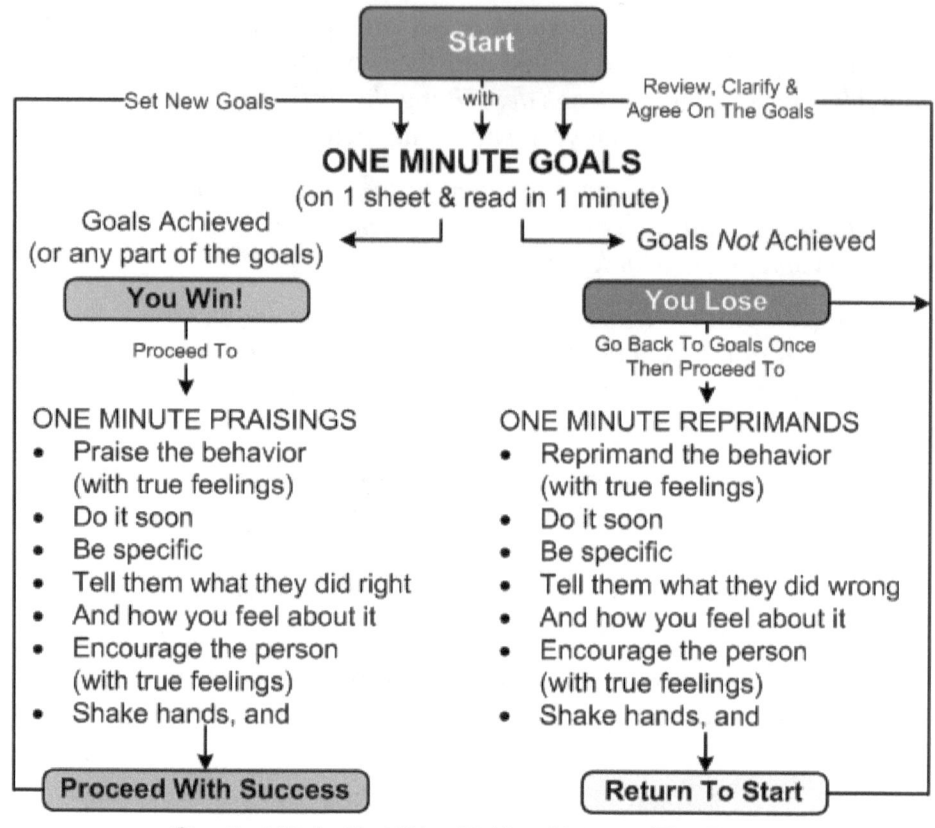

Charlie Mitchell's I Was Taking Notes – The Book

A very brief summary of

THE ONE MINUTE MANAGER'S "GAME PLAN"

How to give yourself and others "the gift" of getting greater results in less time.
SET GOALS; PRAISE & REPRIMAND BEHAVIORS;
ENCOURAGE PEOPLE; SPEAK THE TRUTH; LAUGH; WORK; ENJOY
And encourage the people you work with to do the same as you do!

Atta Boy

The second aspect of one minute managing is one minute praisings:

- Tell people up front that you are going to let them know how they are doing
- Praise people immediately
- Tell people what they did right – be specific

- Tell people how good you feel about what they did right, and how it helps the organization and the other people who work there
- Stop for a moment of silence to let them *feel* how good you feel
- Encourage them to do more of the same
- Shake hands or touch people in a way that makes it clear that you support their success in the organization

Oh Boy

The third part is the one minute reprimands:

1. Tell people beforehand that you are going to let them know how they are doing and in no uncertain terms

The first half of the reprimand:

2. Reprimand people immediately
3. Tell people what they did wrong, be specific
4. Tell people how you feel about what they did wrong - and in no uncertain terms
5. Stop for a few seconds of uncomfortable silence and let them feel how you feel

The second half of the reprimand:

6. Shake hands, or touch them in a way that lets them know you are honestly on their side
7. Remind them how much you value them
8. Reaffirm that you think well of them but not of their performance in this situation
9. Realize that when the reprimand is over, it's over

An effective reprimand requires being honest, fair, clear, prompt and quick. It can take as little as 30 seconds to complete them correctly. Following the reprimand, shake hands and remind the person that he or she is important and it was simply their performance that you did not like. The one minute reprimand consists of the reprimand and the reassurance, both being equally important. If you leave the latter out, you will not be liked by those around you and they will attribute mistakes to them being worthless, which is far from the truth.

Chapter 10 Checklists

A checklist is the simplest form of process documentation.

My Story

My history with checklists goes back to my first job as a customer support engineer at B&K Instruments in the early 1980s. I would get dozens of calls each week and need to follow up most with a letter. There was no way to remember everything without creating a checklist.

Fast forward to the late 1990s when my checklist, on a clear acrylic clipboard with my name engraved on it, had become the hallmark of my personal style. Larry Roloson walked into my office one day when I was talking with someone and without a word, looked around for my clipboard, picked it up and wrote something on it. He put it down and started to walk out. I asked him if he needed something. He answered with a straight face, "No, I know that if I can get something on your check list, it will get done."

Origin

It seems like checklists have always been around, but as history goes, it is a relatively new, post-industrial revolution invention.

Back in 1934, the US Army Air Corp asked three different companies; Boeing, Douglas, and Martin, to each build their own version of a new plane to compete for a contract to build the Army's new bomber. When the planes were done and put through testing, the Boeing model appeared to be the hands-down winner.

But, at the final flight test, the Boeing plane stalled after take-off and crashed because the test flight crew forgot to release an elevator lock.

As a result of the crash, Douglas Aircraft got the bulk of the Army contract which was for 133 planes. Boeing only got an order for 13 planes which were ordered for further testing. The Army was going to watch to see if the Boeing plane really was too much for one man to fly, which was their theory as to why it had crashed.

But the engineers at Boeing were convinced that their plane was *not* too much plane for one man to fly, just too complex for one man to remember all of the necessary steps. So they created four flight procedures in a checklist format.

Using those checklists, the 13 Boeing test planes then flew 1.8 million miles without incident. As a result, the Army ordered over 12,000 planes from Boeing, which saved Boeing from going out of business.

The checklist method proved to be so effective that it was used on the Apollo space program where checklists were attached to spacesuit sleeves during the walk on the surface of the moon.

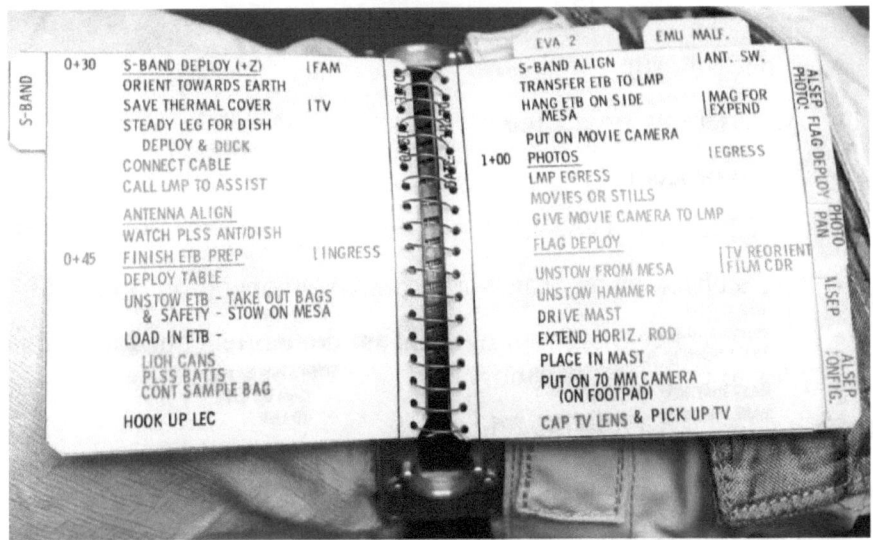

Today, checklists are constantly used around the world in critical safety performance situations.

So what is a checklist? A checklist is:

- a complete list of items,

- or a sequential set of steps,

- or both combined.

As a **complete list of items**, its benefit is that nothing is accidentally forgotten. Once the list is made, you can focus on other tasks, knowing that you won't accidentally forget something as long as you remember to use the list.

As a **sequential list of items**, its benefit is that nothing is performed in the wrong order. Lots of test and assembly operations need to be done in a specific order to work.

A cooking recipe is an example that is a **both** a complete list and a sequential list.

So what else is a checklist?

- A meeting action item list
- A compliance table
- A packing slip
- An assembly procedure
- A test procedure

So when do we need a checklist?

- Use a checklist anytime some *multi-step* operation is critical
- Create a checklist for things that are done often, but are *too complex* to commit to memory

That's it. Here are a few final thoughts:

- Only up-to-date checklists really work well
- There's no single *right* tool for making checklists; use whatever tool works (e.g. spreadsheet, Daytimer, MS-Outlook, notebook, clipboard, whiteboard, mobile phone)
- Whatever you pick, pick a tool that is easy to change so that you can easily treat the list like a *living* document
- Put it in a well-known place so you can always find it and so others can benefit from it
- Remember to use it yourself

Chapter 11 Getting Things Done

Stuff is bouncing around in our heads and causing untold stress and anxiety.

~ David Allen, *Getting Things Done*

Below is a blog post written by Merlin Mann, *Getting started with "Getting Things Done." (September 8, 2004)*

Getting started with *Getting Things Done*

The Problem with Stuff

Getting Things Done (GTD) succeeds because it first addresses a critical barrier to completing the atomic tasks that we want to accomplish in a given day. That's *stuff. Amorphous, unactionable, sweat-inducing stuff.* David says:

> Here's how I define *stuff*: anything you have allowed into your psychological or physical world that doesn't belong where it is, but for which you haven't yet determined the desired outcome and the next action step.

Stuff is bouncing around in our heads and causing untold stress and anxiety. Evaluation meetings, bar mitzvahs, empty rolls of toilet paper, broken lawn mowers, college applications, your big gut, tooth decay, dirty underwear and imminent jury duty all compete for prime attention in our poor, addled brains. *Stuff* has no *home* and, consequently, no place to go, so it just keeps rattling around.

Worse off, we're too neurotic to stop thinking about it, and we certainly don't have time to actually do everything in one day.

So you sprint from fire to fire, praying you haven't forgotten anything, sapped of anything like creativity or even the basic human flexibility to adapt your own schedule to the needs of your friends, your family or yourself. Your *stuff* has taken over your brain like a virus now, dragging down every process it touches and rendering you spent and virtually useless. Sound familiar?

So how does GTD work?

This is a really summarized version, but here it is:

1. Identify all the stuff in your life that isn't in the right place (all open loops)

2. Get rid of the stuff that isn't yours or you don't need right now

3. Create a right place that you trust and that supports your working style and values (e.g., a checklist, folders)

4. Put your stuff in the right place, consistently

5. Do your stuff in a way that honors your time, your energy, and the context of any given moment

6. Iterate and refactor mercilessly

So, basically, you make your stuff into real, actionable items or things you can just get rid of. Everything you keep has a *clear reason* for being in your life at any given moment—both now and well into the future. This gives you an amazing kind of confidence that:

a) Nothing gets lost, and

b) You always understand what's on or off your plate.

Also, built into the system are an ongoing series of reviews, in which you periodically re-examine your now-organized stuff from various levels of granularity to make sure your vertical focus (individual projects and their tasks) is working in concert with your horizontal focus (side to side scanning of all incoming channels for new stuff). It's actually sort of fun and oddly satisfying.

The underlying psychology of *Getting Things Done* is helpful whether or not you use David Allen's organizational techniques. Merlin Mann's *43 Folders* website is a useful resource for this.

Chapter 12 Hyperproductivity and Pomodoros

Everyone can get there, without exception; it's actually not hard at all once you know what to do.

~ Jeff Sutherland
Speaking of hyperproductivity at Open Volcano (2010)

Hyperproductivity

The increased productivity of agile software development teams has come to be called hyperproductivity, which is defined as an increase in a Scrum team's productivity by several hundred percent.

But here, we are concerned with individual, personal productivity, defined as that brief period of time when one is *in-the groove* and able to produce high quality work in a short burst.

When Stephen Covey describes the Important/Non-Urgent quadrant of Eisenhower's Matrix, it is his quadrant 2 which creates the condition where hyperproductivity can occur:

	Urgent	Not Urgent
Important	Quadrant 1	Quadrant 2 Hyperproductivity can occur here
Not important	Quadrant 3	Quadrant 4

*For a more detailed diagram see page 15.

Your Recipe

What will it take to get you into a hyperproductive state? There is no one-size-fits-all solution. You will have to figure out your own recipe for getting into hyperproductivity.

Develop your own specific approach that matches your circumstances. Some things to try include:

- Define the work – (in advance; clearly; know if things you need are missing)

- Block out distractions

- Produce without correcting – Generate raw work as fast as you can, and do not correct as you go.

Pomodoro

The *Pomodoro Technique* is a time management method developed by Francesco Cirillo in the late 1980s. The technique uses a timer to break down work into intervals traditionally 25 minutes in length, separated by short breaks. These intervals are known as *pomodori*, the plural of the Italian word *pomodoro* or *tomato*. The method is based on the idea that frequent breaks can improve mental agility.

The *Pomodoro Technique* is named after the tomato-shaped kitchen timer that was first used by Cirillo when he was a university student.

If you have a large and varied to-do list, using the *Pomodoro Technique* can help you crank through projects faster by forcing you to adhere to strict timing. Watching the timer wind down can spur you to wrap up your current task more quickly, and spreading a task over two or three pomodori can keep you from getting frustrated. The constant timing of your activities makes you more accountable for your tasks, and minimizes the time you spend procrastinating. You'll grow to *respect the tomato*, and that can help you to better handle your workload.

The stages of planning, tracking, recording, processing and visualizing are fundamental to the technique. In the planning phase, tasks are prioritized by recording them in a *To Do Today* list. This enables users to estimate the effort tasks require. As pomodori are completed, they are recorded, adding to a sense of accomplishment and providing raw data for subsequent self-observation and improvement.

There are five basic steps to implementing the technique:

- Decide on the task to be done
- Set the pomodoro timer to N minutes
- Work on the task until the timer rings; record with an x
- Take a short break
- After four pomodori, take a longer break

For the purposes of the technique, *pomodoro* refers to the interval of time spent working. After task completion, any time remaining in the pomodoro is devoted to overlearning. Regular breaks are taken, aiding assimilation. A short (3–5 minute) rest separates consecutive pomodori. Four pomodori form a set. A longer (15–30 minute) rest is taken between sets.

An essential aim of the technique is to reduce the impact of internal and external interruptions on focus and flow. A pomodoro is indivisible. When interrupted during a pomodoro, either the other activity must be recorded and postponed (inform – negotiate – schedule – call back), or the pomodoro must be abandoned.

There are lots of free apps available for pomodoro timers, but the creator and others encourage a low-tech approach, using a mechanical timer, paper and pencil. The physical act of winding up the timer confirms the user's determination to start the task; ticking externalizes desire to complete the task; ringing announces a break. Flow and focus become associated with these physical stimuli.

Chapter 13 Muda, Mura, Muri

Eliminating waste is one of the best ways to improve speed, quality, and reduce cost.

Japanese industrialists are known for having taken quality initiatives and turned them into more than just ways to improve final product quality. They applied this thinking to speed and cost. Taiichi Ohno developed the Toyota production system, which included what we now know as *Lean Manufacturing*. The three problems of *lean* are:

- Muda – Waste
- Mura – Unevenness
- Mari – Overburden

Muda

Muda is work which does not add value. Muda is defined in seven original categories, plus an eighth added later:

1. Transport – movement of product between work centers and locations
2. Inventory – work in progress (WIP), finished goods, and raw materials that a company holds in stock
3. Motion – physical movement of a person or machine performing a manufacturing operation
4. Waiting – waiting for a machine to become available for the waiting WIP, for product to arrive, or any other unproductive delay
5. Overproduction – producing more of a product than what is needed to meet customer demand
6. Over-processing – performing operations beyond those that customer requires (e.g., over polishing)
7. Defects – quality rejects and out of spec work
8. Talent – failing to utilize all of the skills and knowledge of your team

This last has gained general acceptance as part of muda. To these eight, a few people will add:

- Resources – failing to turn off lights and unused machines
- By-Products – not making use of by-products of your process

These can be remembered with the mnemonic "DOWNTIME"

- Defective Production
- Over-production
- Waiting
- Non-used talent
- Transportation
- Inventory
- Motion
- Excessive processing

Mura

Many of these wastes are caused by mura, which is unevenness. Cyclical demand for output causes forces in the manufacturing process which are favorable to waste. It is essential to not have performance metrics (e.g. machine utilization) which accidentally encourage this. A lot of work goes into making manufacturing systems highly responsive to sudden changes in demand, but it is better to smooth out the demand if possible.

Mari

Mari (overburdening) is related, but slightly different. When a system or team is overburdened, its ability to efficiently produce output in compliance with specification is compromised.

Mari is cause by:

- Poor communication and direction

- Unreliable (incapable) processes
- Poor maintenance
- Lack of correct tools
- Incorrect tool setup
- Cluttered or disorganized workspaces
- Insufficient training

All of these aspects of muda, mura, and mari can be combatted with the use of 5S, Six Sigma, TQM, Kanban and similar manufacturing quality systems.

5S

5S is a workplace quality system which stands for

- Sort
- Straighten
- Shine
- Standardize
- Sustain

Part 3 – Communication

Nothing will affect your work more than your
ability to communicate.

Nothing will improve your career more than
learning to write better.

Chapter 14 I Could Care Less (sic)

*People who will never meet you, will read your writing and
form an opinion of you.*

~ Jim Talley, *1989*

Like it or not, your success is influenced by how well you communicate. The content of your message is diminished when you speak or write poorly.

I'll admit that I am a grammar, spelling, and punctuation geek, meaning that I cringe at poorly constructed speech and writing. Here's the thing – everyone is a speech and writing critic to some degree or another. This means that, although you may be willing to let certain errors slide, other errors do bother you. At a minimum, when you see an error, you have thoughts like, "Oh, this person is ignorant," or "This person is lazy." If you find a mistake in a resume, you may discard the document.

Right now you might find yourself looking for errors in this text. Chances are well that you will find them.

In a world where spell checkers pervade, and where any grammatical rule can be Googled in under a minute, the ignorant/lazy assessment is too often accurate.

Here is what happens to readers when your work has errors: They are merrily reading your message, actually grasping the content when *WHAM* they read some typo that interrupts their focus. They then have distracted thoughts about what you did wrong. They think about what the right word or usage would be, they reconsider what you did, they make a judgment about whether it is an appropriate deliberate abuse of language for the given context, they lower their estimation of you, and then finally, they re-engage in your message.

People sometimes justify a poorly written communiqué by saying that the reader can figure out the gist of it with a little effort. But what about the multiplication of effort caused when sending a poorly written email to many people? Doesn't it make sense for the author to make it right once, rather than to have multiple readers struggle with interpreting the meaning? Is your time more valuable than all of theirs? Is your message so unimportant that it does not need to be understood? If you leave it up to the reader to guess your meaning, some will get it wrong.

Count how many times in a workday you observe miscommunication and it will stun you.

Two Minimal Solutions for Better Writing

The easy solution for writing is to turn on the spell checker for all of your word-processing programs. Yes, at first you will have to teach it some custom words like names and acronyms – just do it. My rule of thumb is to always hit (Function) F7 before hitting print or send.

Then read your writing before you publish. This is so easy, yet so many people do not do it. Instead they hit send as soon as they type the last word. Don't do this. Take a moment to read what you wrote. If you send a document with an easy to spot error, people will know how little effort you made.

For Crying Out Loud

Want to write like a pro? Read it out loud. When you read your writing out loud, you engage different parts of the brain than when you only read with your eyes. Speaking the words makes you use the part of your brain that controls speech. Listening makes you use auditory processing parts of the brain. You will find that you can catch errors that have slipped past multiple silent proofreading passes.

Hard Solutions for Speech

Sorry, there are no easy solutions for speech. There is a good chance though, that if you focus on good writing, your speech will improve if you simply try to be well spoken in the same way.

Thinking before you speak is a hard habit to learn. Try it one sentence at a time. Pay attention to how often you start a sentence without knowing how you are going to end it. This is a simple application of Stephen Covey's second habit, "Begin with the end in mind."

Ending with a Preposition

There are modern grammarians who will argue that it is acceptable to end a sentence with a preposition, (e.g. of, to, in, from, for, on, by) but you run the risk of grammar snobs thinking you don't know better if

---

you do it. There is no right answer. A good rule might be to speak that way, but not write that way.

Uptalking

A trend eroding speaker's credibility is ending declarative statements with a rising tone thereby making them sound like a question. This speech pattern, called "uptalk", can be contagious, spreading from one speaker to the next. It is a career-halting habit of which to be cautious. Watch the TED Talk on Uptalk and Vocal Fry.

Planning Ahead

You know this saying: "***Of those to whom much has been given, much will be required.***" You have to plan this sentence to start it correctly. It begins with the word "Of" which is unusual. Can you say it tomorrow without looking?

A Bridge Too Far

Often, we say too many words because they complete familiar sounding phrases. Our ear takes over our mouth.

Here are some examples:

"It was developed in Norway where I spent some time there." The word "there" has no place in this sentence. It just fell out of the speaker's mouth.

"Then we have a presentation online which I don't know what that is." (Senior VP at $22B company. A sentence with more than one subject is always wrong.)

The only cure I know for this is to plan your words before you speak.

Chapter 15 Subject: Check This Out

This email is not important. I only have one thing on my plate. I am discourteous. I do not respect your time. I do not know how to file emails for reference.

~ Lazy Colleague

It's pretty easy to guess that I am not going to condone bad subject lines in business emails. Email has become a significant portion of people's work day so it is essential that it be made productive and efficient. A good subject line should start and improve communication now, and help with finding the email again in the future.

Quiz:

Did you not use a good subject line because:

A. You don't know what you wrote about?

B. Your time is more valuable than mine?

C. You really don't want me to read your email?

D. You don't want me to be able to find it later?

People will evaluate your intelligence and your work by your emails. You can stand above the average by being considerate when writing subject lines.

Think about the initial reading of an email and also think about looking at a long list of old emails, trying to find a specific one from six months ago.

Starting your email with categories like *Request, Info, Delivery, Accepted, and Acknowledged* immediately clue the reader about what to expect.

The name of the client, project, product or whatever major category your business divides work into should be part of every subject line. Even if you only work on one thing at a time (unlikely), the people to whom you are writing probably do not. They should not have to open the email to know what it is about.

You can even put the whole message in the email subject if it is short enough, and if you do, put (EOM) at the end. EOM stands for end-of-message. This way the recipient knows they do not need to open it. If your email requires no response, put (NRN) for no reply needed.

MS-Outlook allows you to edit the subject lines of emails sent to you. Of course this makes following an email thread harder, but if the topic has changed from the original subject, do it and truncate the email at the point where it changed.

Likewise, just because someone sent you an email with a poor subject line does not mean you can't change it when you reply. If they left out important information like the client or project name, add it. When I lead a project, I create a standard six-character or fewer acronym for the project name and ask every team member to start every email for that project with that code.

If your business has standard categories like *proposal, test, training, shop drawings, project plan, schedule* or *installation,* those can be the next part of the subject line. This really helps with searching for old emails. Words like *report* and *meeting* are not narrow enough to be good categories. Don't use them alone.

Here are some examples of bad subject lines we should point at and mock until they are so embarrassed they run out the door crying:

- See attached
- Re: Fwd: Re:
- Check this out
- Pricing
- Proposal
- Tomorrow

MS-Outlook will even allow you to edit the body of an email sent to you. If you are replying to a reply, and spot an error in your original email, why not fix it? When forwarding, you can even fix other people's obvious typos and spare them embarrassment.

Chapter 16 Email Handling

People constantly send me long, unnecessary, and convoluted messages. I get copied on everything. Reply-to-all is out of control.

~ Mike Song, *The Hamster Revolution (2007)*

Email Processing

There are many experts offering opinions on efficiently handling email. Most follow this general approach:

E-mail Processing Method Comparison*			
David Allen *Getting Things Done*		**Stephanie Winston** *Organized for Success*	**Anonymous Technique**
Processing	**Organizing**	**TRAF**	**4 Ds**
Actionable?	Bucket	*Response*	*Response*
N	Trash	Trash	Delete it
N	Someday/Maybe	-	-
N	File	File	-
Y + Delegate	Waiting For	Refer	Delegate
Y + <2 Minutes	Do it	Act	Do (Respond)
Y + >2 Minutes	Defer it (Calendar, Next Actions)	Act	Defer

(c) Charlie Mitchell 2013   * Based on Mathew Cornell's work

Inbox Zero

Inbox Zero is a rigorous approach to email management aimed at keeping the inbox empty almost all of the time. Inbox Zero was developed by productivity expert Merlin Mann. According to Mann, the zero is not a reference to the number of messages in an inbox; it is *the amount of time an employee's brain is in his inbox.* Mann's point is that time and attention are finite and when an inbox is confused with a *to do* list, productivity suffers.

Zero is the amount of time an employee's brain is in his inbox.

Here are some of Mann's tips for effective email management:

- Don't leave the email client open.

- Process email periodically throughout the day, perhaps at the top of each hour.

- First delete or archive as many new messages as possible.

- Then forward what can be best answered by someone else.

- Immediately respond to any new messages that can be answered in two minutes or less.

- Move new messages that require more than two minutes to answer – and messages that can be answered later – to a separate *requires response* folder.

- Set aside time each day to respond to email in the *requires response* folder or chip away at mail in this folder throughout the day.

No Interruptions?

People speak of email and Blackberries like they are some newly invented evil. But are these kinds of urgent, unimportant interruptions new?

Have you ever been at the counter of a retail store, talking to a sales-clerk when the store phone rings? What happens? They immediately interrupt what they are doing and answer it.

We have had the telephone interrupting us for decades. Electronic interruptions are nothing new. Instead of interrupting us by phoning or popping into our offices, people send email. True, some of the email you get is spam, but so were some of the calls and visits you used to get.

Delayed Response

The other piece of common wisdom circulating these days is to set your email so it does not chime every time a new piece of mail arrives. This is so you do not get distracted from tasks which require concentration.

Some extremists only check their mail twice a day in order to protect themselves from interruptions, but that means that you are often leaving your colleagues hanging for hours, waiting for your answers.

How you appear to your manager and colleagues will be affected by how responsive you appear. If you are the last to chime in, you will look slow. If you have a dissenting opinion, it will be heard better at the beginning of an email exchange than at the end.

Don't be in such a hurry to delay reading your email.

Pomodoro It

If you want to turn off your email, do so during your pomodori and turn it on during your breaks. This way you never fall out of communication for more than a half hour.

Filter, Filter, Filter

Being the first to respond to an important email is good; getting interrupted by spam is bad. Take the time to learn how to set up good spam filtering and keep adding to your defenses by marking certain subjects and senders as spam. This will lessen your bad interruptions. A good corporate spam filter will allow one person to review one copy of a suspect email and flag it as spam or not spam for every recipient which is much more efficient than each employee having to open and delete the spam.

Send Less to Get Less

This may not be the best approach to free flowing, good communication, but it is a truth that should be mentioned. If you send less mail, you will get less mail. Certainly you should think twice before sending an email to make sure it is needed, but beware of *dropping out* of a conversation when you should be contributing.

> The team's productivity is more important than yours.

Chapter 17 Eats, Shoots, and Leaves

"A panda walks into a cafe. He orders a sandwich, eats it, then draws a gun and fires two shots in the air.

"Why?" asks the confused waiter, as the panda makes towards the exit. The panda produces a badly punctuated wildlife annual and tosses it over his shoulder.

"I'm a panda," he says, at the door. "Look it up."

The waiter turns to the relevant entry and, sure enough, finds an explanation.

Panda. Large black-and-white bear-like mammal, native to China. Eats, shoots and leaves."

~ Lynne Truss, Eats, Shoots & Leaves: The Zero Tolerance Approach to Punctuation (2003)

I Love This Book

Occasionally people will argue that written English at some point in the past did not have any punctuation and that long before that it did not even have any spaces between words and that therefore it is not necessary to use proper punctuation. While those might be interesting historical facts, it does not excuse a modern English writer from writing in the modern style in order to communicate well.

Capitalization, punctuation, correct word choice, grammar and syntax are all important contributors to effective written communication.

One Subject

The correct number of subjects in a sentence is one. "The dog, he barked," sounds wrong to everyone, but add a few words after the noun dog, and some people feel compelled to use another noun.

Misunderstood and Mispronounced

You can often slide by in speech with slightly mispronounced words and phrases. Failing to conjugate verbs with the correct tense or to manage plural and singular forms of word can often be glossed over for verbal communication, but these stand out like sore thumbs in writing.

Grammar

- These/these ones (the word these means "the ones")
- I couldn't/could care less (if you can care less, you care)
- Imply/infer (a listener infers what a speaker implies)
- Fewer/less (if you can count them, use "fewer")
- Past/passed (A date has passed. That date is in the past.)

Word Order Matters

Not all are does not mean the same thing as *All are not*. When someone says, *Everyone can't be a rocket scientist,* they may be trying to communicate that it is not feasible for everyone to be a rocket scientist, but their words mean that there are no rocket scientists at all, which is clearly not true. Instead, one should say, *Not everyone can be a rocket scientist.*

Let's eat Grandma!

Let's eat, Grandma!

Correct punctuation saves lives

Frequent Pronunciation Errors

Pronunciation

- For/Fur
- To/Ta
- You/Ya
- Accept/Assept
- Known/No-in
- Strength/Strenth
- Success/Sussess

- Whole other/whole nuther
- Should have/should of
- Often/Off-tin
- Intents and purposes/intensive purposes
- Supposed to/suppose to
- Among/Amongst

Chapter 18 Made to Stick

A lie can travel halfway round the world while the truth is putting on its shoes.

~ Charles Haddon Spurgeon,
Sermon, Sunday morning, April 1, 1855

Catchy

Chip and Dan Heath wrote a really cool book, *Made to Stick*, about what makes some stories and marketing messages *stick*, while others, even if part of massive advertising campaign, fail to resonate with their target audiences. In their book, the Heaths' describe six key principles for how to communicate your message so that it *sticks*.

It has the obligatory acronym - SUCCESs, lacking one S:

1. Simplicity – Striping ideas to their core so they are easy to remember (see next chapter for more)

2. Unexpectedness – Avoiding predictability in your statements

3. Concreteness – Using specific details to help people understand and remember ideas

4. Credibility – Doing what is necessary to make your story believable

5. Emotion – Ensuring that others care about your ideas by making them feel something

6. Stories – Getting people to relate to and act on your ideas

Curse of Knowledge

One thing that inhibits people from crafting simple messages is the curse of knowledge. The curse of knowledge occurs when the speaker cannot put themselves in the position of the audience because they are too familiar with the situation and assume information which is not evident. This happens frequently to experienced managers. They know too much!

The curse of knowledge can keep you from creating a simple, good message as is found in this excerpt of JFK's speech about putting a man on the moon:

> *I believe that this nation should commit itself to achieving the goal, before this decade is out, of landing a man on the moon and returning him safely to the earth. No single space project in this period will be more impressive to mankind, or more important for the long-range exploration of space.*
>
> *~ President Kennedy,*
> Address to Congress on Urgent National Needs,
> *(May 25, 1961)*

Read *Made to Stick* to understand how *A lie can travel halfway round the world while the truth is putting on its shoes*. This book has lots of great stories and is a fun read. You'll find out about the guy who gets his kidney stolen, and the truth about razors in Halloween candy.

Chapter 19 Commander's Intent

A clear and concise expression of the purpose of the operation and the desired military end state that supports mission command, provides focus to the staff, and helps subordinate and supporting commanders act to achieve the commander's desired results without further orders, even when the operation does not unfold as planned.

~ US Military Doctrine Manual JP 3-0

Simple Plans

A good example of Chip and Dan Heath's simplicity principle is the US Army's doctrine of *Commander's Intent*. The *Commander's Intent* is a crisp, plain talk instruction used for military instruction. It clearly describes the purpose and desired end state. It has a connection to a business's need for identifying the *single most important thing* that Pat Lencioni describes in *The Five Dysfunctions of a Team*.

Application of *Commander's Intent*

This section of the *US Military Doctrine Manual* explains the use of the commander's intent in support of the doctrine of *Decisive Action*.

> 2-10. Decisive action begins with the commander's intent and concept of operations. As a single, unifying idea, decisive action provides direction for the entire operation. Based on a specific idea of how to accomplish the mission, commanders and staffs refine the concept of operations during planning. They adjust it throughout the operation as subordinates develop the situation or conditions change. Often, subordinates acting on the higher commander's intent develop the situation in ways that exploit unforeseen opportunities.
>
> Commander's intent is a clear and concise expression of the purpose of the operation and the desired military end state that supports mission command, provides focus to the staff, and helps subordinate and supporting commanders act to achieve the commander's desired results without further orders, even when the operation does not unfold as planned (JP 3-0). Mission command requires commanders to convey a clear commander's

intent and concept of operations. These become essential in operations where multiple operational and mission variables interact with the lethal application of ground combat power. Such dynamic interaction often compels subordinate commanders to make difficult decisions in unforeseen circumstances.

Plans are Worthless

Churchill and Eisenhower were both credited with saying *Plans are worthless, planning is invaluable*, acknowledging that once battle begins, plans are immediately in need of revision.

The point of *Commander's Intent* is that it gives people a clear sense of the objective being sought so that they can make their own plans or adaptations in support of the *big idea*. It articulates the purpose and the end state.

When giving instruction, provide this kind of insight to your team, and they will have to come back to you less for guidance and input.

You Have the Right

When instructions are being given to you, feel free to ask, *What is the ultimate objective?* This will keep you from making bad assumptions and mistakes.

One Minute Goal Setting, from Ken Blanchard's, *One Minute Manager,* describes a good method for doing this:

1. Agree on your goals
2. See what good behavior looks like
3. Write out each of your goals on a single sheet of paper using less than 250 words
4. Read and re-read each goal, which requires only a minute or so each time you do it
5. Take a minute every once in a while out of your day to look at your performance and see whether or not your behavior matches your goal

You are completely within your rights to ask for clear instruction from the people giving you direction. Don't feel like it is your fault if you go away and what you thought was clear suddenly is not. This is common-place. You may find there are details about the work that were not evident when you were getting the assignment.

In fact, feel free to say, *Okay, I think I've got it, you want X, Y, and Z. If I have any questions, can I come back for clarification?* Who can say no to that?

Clarity allows things to be done twice as fast at half the cost.

Chapter 20 Conversation

I know you think you understand what you thought I said but I'm not sure you realize that what you heard is not what I meant.

~ Author Unclear

Importance

I believe that wars are created more by miscommunication than for any other reason.

The Hard Easy-Fix

The number one simplest communication problem to fix is very common: we avoid talking to the person we need to talk to. We hint, tell others, ridicule, gossip, manipulate, act surprised, act disappointed; in fact, we do everything but talk to the person we need to talk to.

When we need someone to know something, we need to not practice telepathy, instead:

- Say it aloud
- Say it clearly
- Say it to the person you need to talk to

Make it a point of pride to talk to the person you have an issue with before grumbling to anyone else about their behavior. It is very hard to do.

Six Key Steps to Meaningful Conversation:

1. Identifying the real subject of the conversation for both of you
2. Agreeing on the history
3. Agreeing on what the facts of the situation are
4. Interpreting the history of the "why and how" of those facts
5. Identifying your emotional reaction
6. Determining a course of action

When doing this, make sure you know when you are *telling* and when you are *asking*. We mix them up all the time in order to manipulate.

Switch Modes

For an important conversation, consciously switch into accurate communication mode. We spend so much of our day having sloppy, inefficient conversations, laden with misunderstanding that it is easy to continue in that mode even when having a crucial conversation.

Like active listening, accurate communication can be turned on for a given conversation. Just tell yourself that is what you are going to do and be determined not to walk away without having gotten accurate understanding. Ask yourself if it went well before you depart. If not, fix it.

Telling or Asking

All conversation is a mixture of inquiry and advocacy. This is normal human behavior. Just be aware when you are doing it. Our conversations can be thought of in two dimensions, like this:

	- Inquiry +	
+ **Advocacy** **-**	**Telling** - Dictating - Asserting - Explaining	**Generating** - Skillful discussion - Dialogue - Politicking
	Observing - Bystanding - Sensing - Withdrawing	**Asking** - Interrogating - Interviewing - Clarifying

A Simple Trick

Ask the other person, *Did I ask the right question?* You'll be amazed how this elicits useful information.

> If you are having anxiety about having a discussion, that is a sign that you need to have a deliberate conversation.

Chapter 21 Draw It

Any problem can be made clearer with a picture, and any picture can be created using the same set of tools and rules.

~ Dan Roam, *The Back of the Napkin (2008)*

Why Draw?

Not everything is best communicated with the spoken word. And slide presentations don't always get the job done. Drawing can help you. Right up front it can help you define what your problem is. Drawing allows us to do visual thinking which can stimulate different (otherwise unused) parts of the brain. The fact is that to fully comprehend, solve, and communicate, we *need both* words and images.

Anyone Can Draw

Dan Roam teaches that anyone can draw sufficiently well to help communicate an idea. Basic shapes like circles, rectangles, arrows, stick-figures are enough.

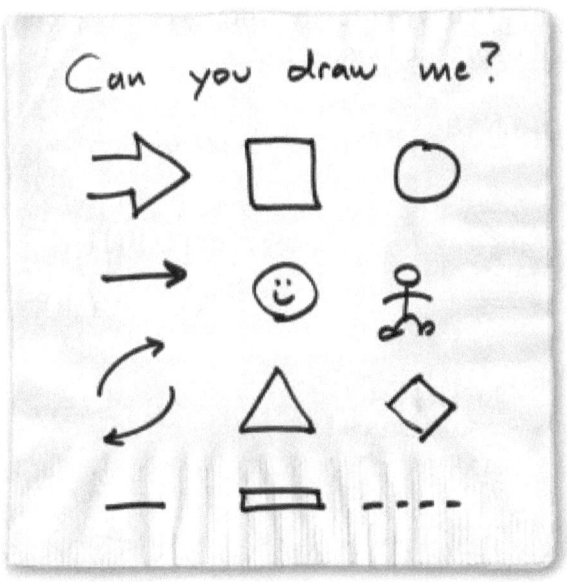

Dan Roam's "Can You Draw Me?" challenge from *The Back of the Napkin*

Three Built-In Tools

You have the basic tools already built-in: your eyes, your mind's eye, and your hands. The only accessories you need are a pencil and paper or a marker and whiteboard. You do not want to use a computer for communicating while drawing. That's right, *while* drawing.

How to Draw to Clarify Problems

When we do visual thinking to solve a problem, we do four things:

Look ⇨ See ⇨ Imagine ⇨ Show

Dan Roam teaches that to look and see, we must:

1. Collect everything we can to look at–the more the better (at least at first).

2. Have a place where we can lay out everything and really look at it, side by side.

3. Always define a basic coordinate system to give us a clear orientation and position.

4. Find ways to cut ruthlessly from everything our eyes bring in— we need to practice visual triage.

Who/What, How Many, Where and When

Having looked and seen with our eyes, we now need to see with our imagination by categorizing the situation by describing it in terms of *Who/What, How Many, Where*, and *When* in order to get to *How*.

What Do I Want to Know? – The SQVID Questions

	S. simple / elaborate	Q. quality / quantity	V. vision / execution	I. individual / comparison	△. change / as-is
1 who/what? (portrait)					
2 how much? (chart)					
3 where? (map)					
4 when? (timeline)					
5 how? (flowchart)					
6 why? (plot)					

Read Dan Roam's book to understand these summary charts.

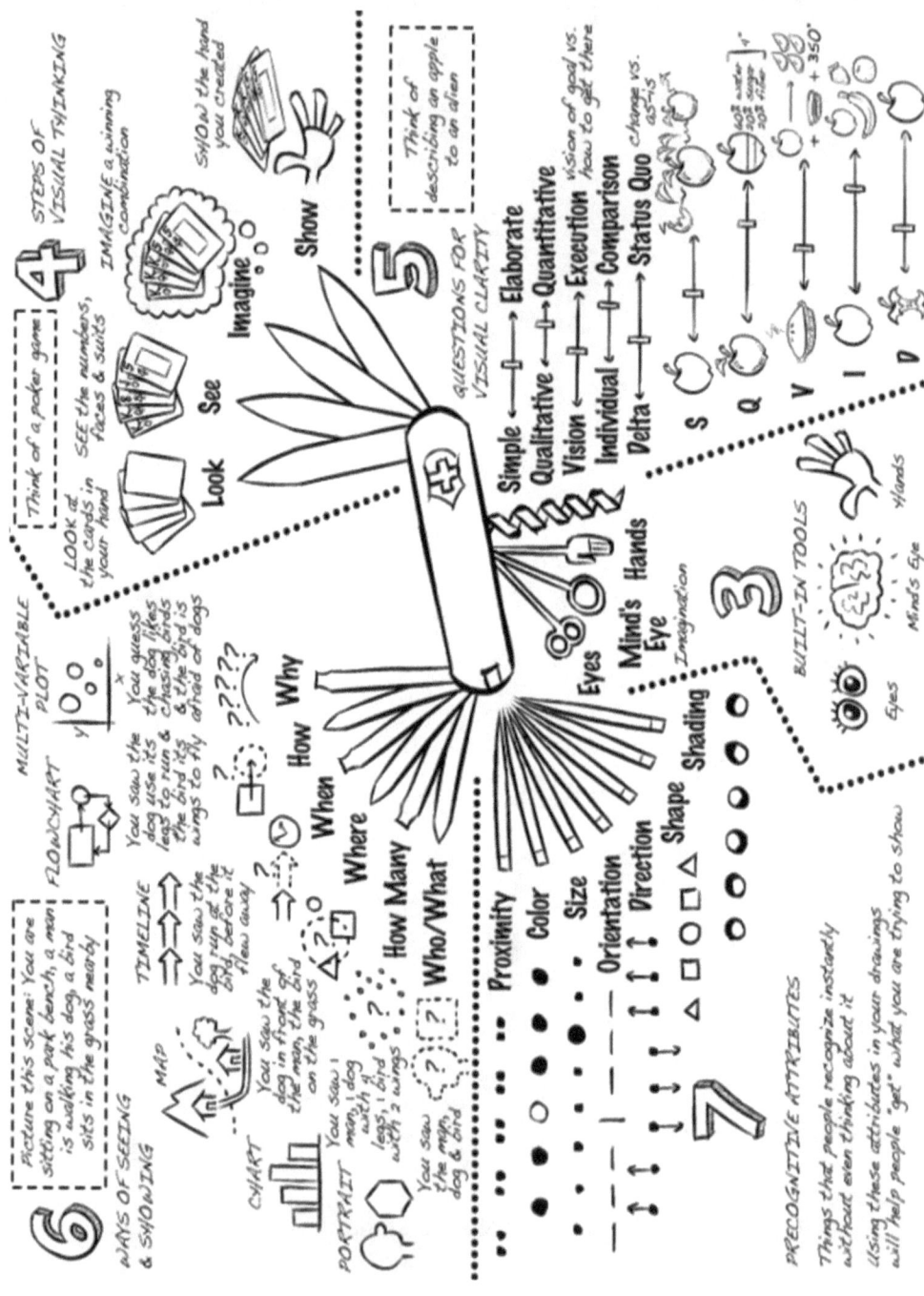

STEPS OF VISUAL THINKING

Look
See
Imagine
Show

Think of a poker game!
LOOK at the cards in your hand
SEE the numbers, faces & suits
IMAGINE a winning combination
SHOW the hand you created

QUESTIONS FOR VISUAL CLARITY

Simple → Elaborate
Qualitative → Quantitative
Vision → Execution
Individual → Comparison
Delta → Status Quo

Think of describing an apple to an alien

Elaborate
Quantitative
Execution — vision of goal vs. how to get there
Comparison
Status Quo — change vs. as-is

S
Q
V
I
D

BUILT-IN TOOLS

Eyes
Mind's Eye — Imagination
Hands

Eyes
Mind's Eye
Hands

Why
How
When
Where
How Many
Who/What

Eyes
Mind's Eye
Hands

Proximity
Color
Size
Orientation
Direction
Shape
Shading

PRECOGNITIVE ATTRIBUTES

Things that people recognize instantly without even thinking about it

Using these attributes in your drawings will help people "get" what you are trying to show

WAYS OF SEEING & SHOWING

MAP

CHART

PORTRAIT — You saw 1 man, 1 dog with 4 legs, 1 bird with 2 wings

You saw the map's dog & bird

MULTI-VARIABLE PLOT

FLOWCHART

TIMELINE

You saw the dog run in front of the man, the bird on the grass

You guess the dog likes to run & chase birds & the bird is afraid of dogs

You saw the dog run in front of the bird before it flew away

Picture this scene: You are sitting on a park bench, a man is walking his dog, a bird sits in the grass nearby

Part 4 – Meetings

Make the time you spend with others productive.

Chapter 22 Modern Meeting Standard

Meetings are the place momentum goes to die.

~ Al Pittampalli, *Read This Before Our Next Meeting (2011)*

Meetings – Ugh

In many companies, meetings are not only prevalent, they occupy the most productive periods of the week. There are some senior executives who believe that meetings are their primary job function. And since many meetings are scheduled electronically via MS-Outlook by administrative assistants, people find their calendars packed with back-to-back meetings where the agenda is unknown and sometimes even the meeting owner is unknown. As a result, people show up unprepared.

Having shown up unprepared, the meetings are then poorly run, wandering imprecisely, failing to resolve one issue before accidentally meandering onto the next topic. A few vague assignments get made, no clear decisions get made, and no accountability structure exists to ensure that assignments get completed on time.

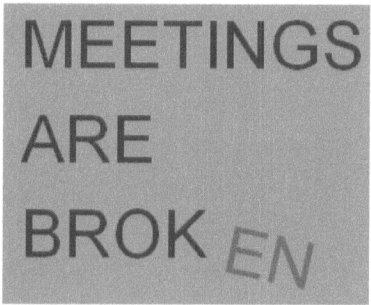

Yep – meetings are broken.

Al Pittampalli, author of *Read This Before Our Next Meeting,* puts forth the need for a fundamentally different approach for what he calls the *"Modern Meeting"* to making meetings productive. Here is an excerpt from his website describing his manifesto for what a meeting should be:

Manifesto

The Modern Meeting:

1. Exists only to support a decision that has already been made. A traditional meeting discourages people from deciding. Meetings are weapons of mass-interruption. When you have a decision to make, go ahead and get input from people, but do it in advance, one-on-one, then make the decision. Once you make the decision, you may not need the meeting. If you do have the meeting, the purpose is to vet the decision. Be willing to change your mind. This is a much more powerful way to hold a meeting. It has a bias toward action.

2. Starts on schedule, moves fast, and ends on schedule. That is to optimize the decision. Hard deadlines help.

3. Limits the number of attendees. Consensus is a myth. Groups are great at disagreeing, but poor at agreeing.

4. Rejects the unprepared. If you come unprepared, you lose.

5. Produces committed action plan. This is the point: deciding to do something.

6. Refuses to be informational. Reading memos beforehand is mandatory.

7. Works alongside a culture of brainstorming. We often treat brainstorming like a meeting. It is not a meeting. Make brainstorming fun and unconstrained.

Remember - Anyone can call a mediocre meeting.

Three Meeting Keystones

1. Identify one decision owner *before* **any decision-oriented meeting convenes.** When team members' responsibility is ambiguous, which happens when you involve a lot of people, they perform worse. Leadership is the antidote to the bystander effect. Once one person tips a street performer, others will join in.

2. Replace meetings with one-on-one conversations. This produces amazing cascading effects because you have to really think about who you need to talk to. It increases quality and reduces cost.

3. Make all standing meetings tentative. Go ahead and let people book the time on their calendars so the meeting can happen, but force someone to actively decide that they have a good enough reason to spend the money on the meeting. If you have a meeting where the first order of business is to decide what to cover, you have institutionalized the meeting. If you have a meeting where you cover virtually the same status every time, you have institutionalized a meeting.

Relationship to *The Five Dysfunctions of a Team*

This ties to Pat Lencioni's, *The Five Dysfunctions of a Team,* which directly connects to behavior before, during, and after meetings. At a productive meeting, people:

- Say what they truly feel and know, instead of speaking for effect (political motives).

- Have productive conflict in meetings, arguing productively to get all aspects of an issue out into public debate.

- Are specific about what decisions are being made. And each attendee should be prepared to communicate that decision to their organization.

- Hold each other accountable to uphold and implement decisions made at meetings. Lack of follow through (by anyone) should not be acceptable (to anyone).

- Need to put the organization's needs above individual, department, project, or product needs.

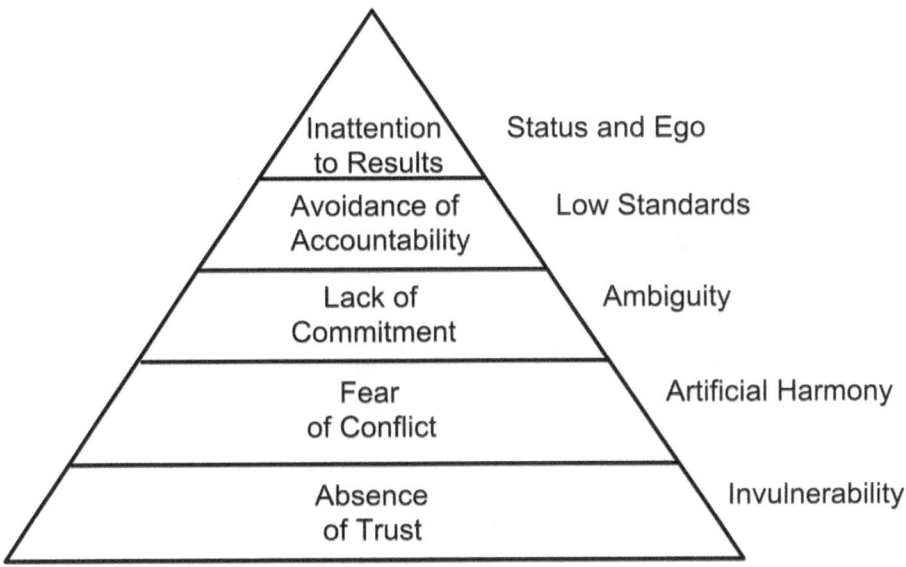

Pointers

- Never have a meeting without an agenda published in advance.

- If the meeting is being set up by an administrative assistant, the invitation should state who the meeting owner is. This is the person accepting responsibility for the cost of the attendee's time.

- Be explicit about who mandatory attendees are and who optional attendees are. If the mandatory attendees can't make it, postpone the meeting. If you can have the meeting without them, they're not mandatory.

- Put all meeting info (e.g., bridge numbers, WebEx, files) in the original invitation. Don't say you'll send it later.

- For an electronic meeting invitation, put in the bridge phone number with commas as pauses before the access code so it can be recognized and automatically dialed from a Smart Phone with a single touch. This is extremely convenient for people who are traveling and can really help when you're in a hurry (e.g., +18665551212,,,12345678).

Chapter 23 Brainstorming Sessions

*Meetings are for making decisions, brainstorming sessions
are to hatch new ideas, discuss constraints, test theories
and get feedback on ideas.*

Team Brainstorming

Brainstorming is the process of collecting ideas without filtering, not allowing anyone to critique an idea until all of the ideas have been generated. There should be no judgment of the merit of any one idea, nor should there be any explanation of why an idea will not work. There should not even be the criticism that a new idea is essentially a restatement of a previous idea.

The only reaction to an idea permitted is to let it trigger the next idea, continuing this way until the maximum number of ideas has been collected. Any hint of disapproval, even jokingly, will impede the flow of ideas, especially from timid participants. Brainstorming should continue until each participant has exhausted their imagination.

Very few teams can pull this off.

Tom Kelley's Seven Secrets for Better Brainstorming:

Tom Kelly, author of "The Art of Innovation," describes seven repeatable techniques for effective brain storming:

1. Begin with a well-honed statement of the problem.

- Gets the brainstorm running with a clear objective

- Allows you to bring the team back to the main topic easily

- *Go for something tangible participants can sink their teeth into, without limiting the possible solutions*

2. Have playful rules. Make sure to put the brainstorming rules predominantly somewhere in the room so everyone can see them.

- Don't critique or debate ideas

- Go for quantity

- Encourage wild ideas

- Be visual

3. Number your ideas.

A hundred ideas per hour usually indicated a good, fluid brainstorming session.

- It is used as a motivational tool

- It can be used to measure progress

- It is a great way to jump back and forth from idea to idea without losing track of your place

4. Build and jump.

High energy brainstorms tend to follow a series of steep 'power' curves. Effective facilitators can recognize these curves and know how to channel the attention and activities of the brainstorming team when their energy and momentum begins to plateau. This may be done by either:

- Jumping back to an earlier path or idea you skipped by too quickly

- Building the idea further in attempt to reach the next power curve

5. Utilize the power of spatial memory

While there are numerous IT solutions for group ideation, Kelley believes that simple tactile tools like markers, sticky notes, and butcher paper are the most successful.

As a facilitator, *write the flow of ideas down in a medium visible to the whole group.*

A visual display of ideas allows your team to see the progress they have made and helps facilitators quickly jump to ideas that seem worthy of more attention.

As you rapidly capture the team's ideas, make mental note of the ones that are worth coming back to during a build or jump. When you return to a spot on the wall where that idea was captured, spatial memory will help people recapture the mindset they had when the idea first emerged.

6. Mental warm-ups

Required? Not necessarily in all circumstances, but mandatory if:

- The group has not worked together before
- The majority of team members do not incorporate brainstorming into their day-to-day activities
- The group seems distracted by pressing but unrelated issues

Additional practices Tom mentions in passing are:

- Assigning content-related homework
- Bringing wide variety of options and materials that could be applied to a session's topic. (e.g., *show and tell*)
- Field trips

7. Get Physical

The basic brainstorm activities are visual: sketching, mind mapping, and diagramming. Kelley stresses, however, that the most rewarding brainstorms push the third dimension. Doing this requires the facilitator to:

- *Bring everything but the kitchen sink* to the brainstorm including; competitive products, solutions from other fields, and emerging technologies.
- Have materials on hand to build crude prototypes (e.g., Legos).
- Allow team members to act out behaviors or actions through skits and scenarios.

Tips and Tricks

The optimum length for a brainstorming session is 60 minutes, but in some cases, may productively stretch to an hour and a half. Kelley argues that *the level of physical and mental energy required for a brainstorm is hard to sustain for much longer than that.*

Think of products in terms of verbs rather than nouns– not cell phones, but cell phoning. An advantage of this practice is that it does not focus on the technology but rather the value or ability it provides the user.

This practice helps you to cross pollinate different product characteristics by combining their values and functions into stronger solutions for the lead user.

Six Ways to Kill a Brainstorm

1. Have the boss speak first. *When the boss begins by setting an agenda and boundaries, your brainstorm is immediately limited.*

2. Insist that everybody gets a turn.

3. Limit team members to experts only.

4. Conduct the brainstorm off-site.

5. Don't allow the *silly stuff.*

6. Write everything down.

Early Dismissal

If someone criticizes an idea after the ground rules for no critiquing has been explained, ask them to leave the room. This will seem very severe, but it is the only way to preserve the non-judgment tone. It sends a powerful message to the whole team. You will likely only ever have to do this once. People will talk about it. The bad behavior will not be repeated.

The person will protest and promise to do better, but what has been done cannot be undone. It is best to explain this beforehand.

I Was Taking Notes

Part 5 – Management

Culture eats strategy for breakfast.

~ Peter Drucker

Chapter 24 Name the Problem to Solve It

When a problem comes along, you must whip it.

~ Mark Mothersbaugh and Gerald V. Casale *(1980)*

Name That Tune

The 80's band Devo wrote, *When a problem comes along, you must whip it.*

I say, *When a problem comes along, you must call it out. Name it.*

This is the first step to solving any problem.

Flag it as belonging to a category. By defining it as belonging to a group or type, you have instantly and immediately begun the solving process in an easier way.

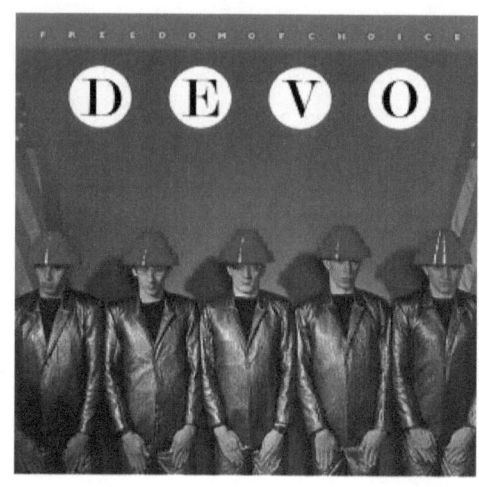

What is new (to us) is the mental handle we can use to wield the idea.

Categories and mental handles are great.

Disempower It

Often, this simple process of giving a problem a name of your choosing neutralizes its ability to hold you in fear.

If not, ask, *What's the worst that could happen?* If you realize that you will survive it, suddenly you can focus on solving it.

Solving Problems

Most of us take a *fuzzy* approach to problem solving. We mull it over and wait for an idea to come to us, and then we run with the first idea. We do this because it works most of the time. But how often have you later on said, *I wish I'd thought of this other idea instead,* or later had someone else suggest an idea that you would not have thought of?

We can change the way we solve important problems by applying a few simple steps. Not every problem is difficult enough to merit a structured approach, but when you have a tough problem it is worth trying a structured problem solving technique. Sometimes the result can be almost magical.

There are a number of structured problem solving techniques, and there is no single one that works all the time. Most of them work because they deconstruct the problem into *pieces* which exposes the *causes*. Once there is clarity about the real parts of the problem and the causes, solutions become much easier to identify. Here is an easy, sample process:

- Name it and tell people the name (this step works like magic somehow, perhaps because we finally accept that the problem is real and not going away by itself)

- Define it:
    - What is happening? (these should be facts)
    - What should be happening? (this is a specific goal) (See Blanchard's, *The One Minute Manager*, chapter 8)

- What does it impact? (this can be opinion)

- Who owns the problem? (this creates accountability)

Once you have identified these basic aspects of the problem, it becomes very easy to invent and evaluate solutions. When someone suggests a solution, immediately ask how well it addresses the, *What should be happening?* part of the problem. Many poor solutions will only solve one facet of a problem. Stating what it fails to address allows you to develop a solution for that facet, and then eventually synthesize a complete solution.

The Toyota *Five-Whys* method can help uncover the root cause. After each answer, ask why again, until you get to the root.

The Ishikawa *Fishbone* diagram method can help you to understand multiple causes which can then be ranked with a *Pareto Chart*.

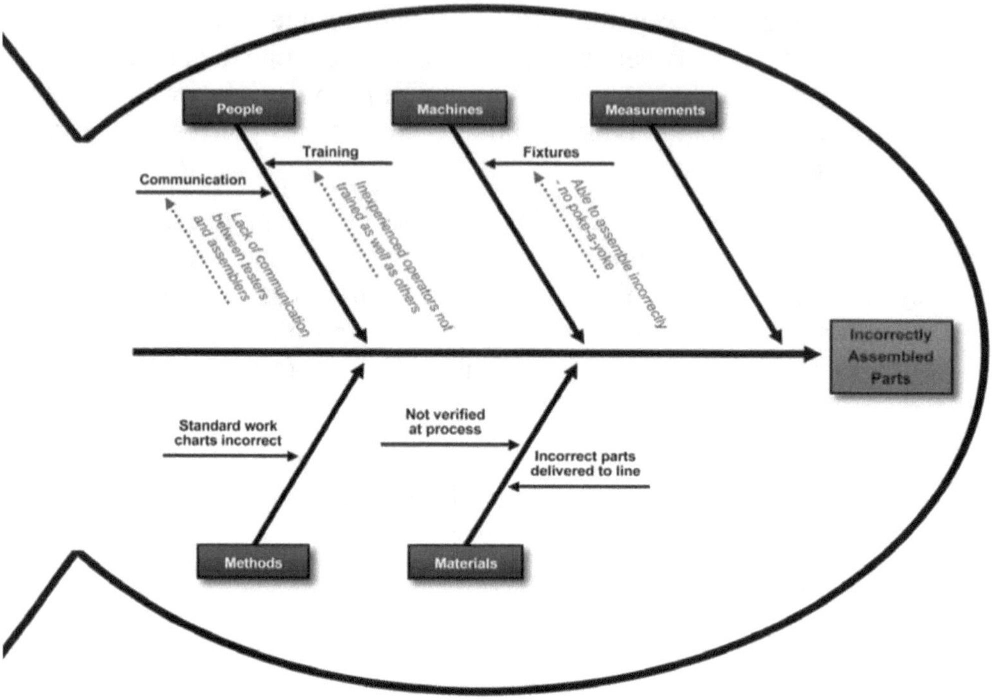

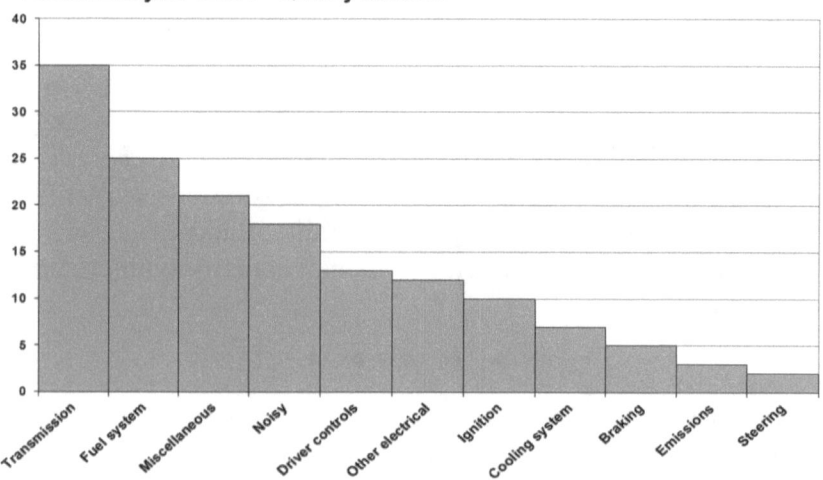

Ishakawa Cause Diagram

Pareto Chart

Chapter 25 Management Quotes

If I have seen further, it is by standing on the shoulders of giants.

~ Sir Isaac Newton,
In a letter to Robert Hooke in February 1676

Risk

People who don't take risks generally make about two big mistakes a year. People who do take risks generally make about two big mistakes a year.

~ Peter Drucker

Teamwork

Not finance. Not strategy. Not technology. It is teamwork that remains the ultimate competitive advantage, both because it is so powerful and so rare.

~ Patrick Lencioni,
The Five Dysfunctions of a Team

People

The team with the best players usually does win - this is why you need to invest the majority of your time and energy in developing your people.

~ Jack Welch, GE CEO

Reputation

It takes 20 years to build a reputation and five minutes to ruin it. If you think about that, you'll do things differently.

~ Warren Buffett

Bad Management

Most of what we call management consists of making it difficult for people to get their work done.

~ Peter Drucker

Talking to Reporters

Nothing is ever off the record. ~ Dennis Moore, DM Strategies

Long Range Plans Meaningless

It is meaningless to speak of short-range and long-range plans. There are plans that lead to action today - and they are true plans, true strategic decisions. And there are plans that talk about action tomorrow - they are dreams, if not pretexts for nonthinking, nonplanning, and nondoing.

~ Peter Drucker

Ask Yourself

Ask yourself these three questions on a regular basis:

- *What am I not saying that needs to be said?*
- *What am I saying that's not being heard?*
- *What's being said that I'm not hearing?*

~ Rob Cromer, CEO of Adcade

Projects and Lawyers

When was the last time you saw a lawyer getting involved in a project dispute make it go faster, better, or cost less? So tell me again why we involve lawyers?

~ Joe Ely, *2005*

Things Left Unsaid

Things left unsaid are always better when they are said clearly.

~ Jean-Philippe Favre
Software Development Manager, *2015*

Investing More

Sunk costs are real, but when making a new decision, they're immaterial. This is the beginning. Again

~ Seth Godin
Seth's Blog, December 19, 2016

Be, Do, Have

So often when people want to start a business, people run out and rent office space and print business stationery, but that is backwards. It is like when a professional ballet dancer starts by buying shoes and an outfit, but the Prima Ballerina knows she is a ballerina long before she has the trappings. First you must be the thing you want, then do the work, then last have the physical things.

~ Malcolm Pancoast, *1993*

Bad System

A bad system will beat a good person every time.
~ W. Edwards Deming

Other Customers

Never tell a customer that you cannot do their work now because you are working on another customer's job.
~ Phil Weinstein, *1994*

Column A and B

A successful business leader needs competency in finance and one of these areas: leadership, technology, sales, or operations. Without financial literacy, you cannot succeed in running a company.

~ Joe Ely, *2001*

Informal Education

Formal education is a foundation, but lifelong, informal education can transform our lives. And informal education scales. It spreads more easily than ever before. Educated people create other educated people. The standards go up when education is present, because the cost of being the least educated person in your tribe is high.

Ignorance, on the other hand, can spread as well. When the cultural dynamic in your circle is that ignorance is prized, it will pull others down and lead to more ignorance.

~ Seth Godin
Seth's Blog, November 13, 2016

Secrets

Never let someone pen you in by telling you that you must keep a secret. Simply tell them to either trust you to use the information responsibly, or not tell you at all.

~ Pete Shults, *2016*

Innovation

You cannot be both efficient and creative at the same time.

~ Pat Lencioni, Blog, *2009*

History

Those who cannot remember the past are condemned to repeat it.

~ George Santayana
The Life of Reason, 1905

Change Mind

Sure, I decided that then, when I knew what I knew then. And if the facts were still the same, my decision would be too. But the facts have changed. We've all heard them. New facts mean it's time for me to make a new decision, without regard for what I was busy doing yesterday, without concern for the people who might disagree with me. My guess is that once they realize these new facts, they're likely to make the same new decision I just did. This decision is more important than my pride.

~ Seth Godin
Seth's Blog, October 20, 2016

Hardest Thing in Business

The hardest thing to do in business is not to set priorities; it is choosing the non-priority to sacrifice. Any fool can identify priorities.

~ Charlie Mitchell, *2016*

Jerks

If an employee at your organization walked out with a brand-new laptop every day, you'd have him arrested, or at least fired. If your bookkeeper was embezzling money every month, you'd do the same thing.

But when an employee demoralizes the entire team by undermining a project, or when a team member checks out and doesn't pull his weight, or when a bully causes future stars to quit the organization—too often, we shrug and point out that this person has tenure, or vocational skills or isn't so bad. But they're stealing from us.

~Seth Godin
It's Your Turn Blog, January 21, 2017

Chapter 26 Being a Better Manager

'Nine Minutes on Monday' is designed to help you trans-form your leadership slowly, implementing small steps.

~ James Robbins, *Nine Minutes on Monday*

Three Facts

- A manager is paid to produce results, but their people, not they themselves, actually produce the results.

- Leadership makes all the difference.

- Leadership is a practice.

Four Needs

Primary four needs of an employee:

- Care – the need to be more than a number

- Mastery – the need for challenge and achievement

- Recognition – the need to be appreciated

- Purpose – the need to contribute and be significant

Nine Questions

In *Nine Minutes on Monday*, James Robbins identified nine questions to help focus you on one of the four needs, and help you plan how you can spend time in the week ahead making progress with one or more of your staff members:

Minute 1: How will I take a genuine interest in my employees this week? This might involve a 15-minute walkabout to chat with staff, or remembering to check in with a staff member returning today from two weeks of tending to a sick mother.

Minute 2: To whom will I give feedback to this week? James Robbins calls feedback the Midas touch, because people crave the right kind of feedback and it can turn them into gold.

Minute 3: Who will I reward or recognize this week? He notes that opportunities for reward and recognition are like birthdays; they have to be recognized immediately or the belated wishes are stale.

Minute 4: To whom will I give the *second paycheck* to this week, helping them to understand the purpose of their work? Purpose is a second paycheck, motivating people more than their real paycheck.

Minute 5: How can I help someone grow this week?

Minute 6: How can I promote a feeling of autonomy in one employee this week? Asking yourself, *Whom will I help feel autonomous?* flies in the face of so many managers who think they must control every aspect of their employees' performance. If they are managing the department, they must have their hand in every little thing.

But, this level of micro-management tends to destroy morale and results in your good employees leaving and your bad employees doing just enough to not get fired. We crave autonomy and the ability to make choices. Having flexibility to do it your way results in more engaged and more productive employees. Use the *Commander's Intent* to provide guard rails.

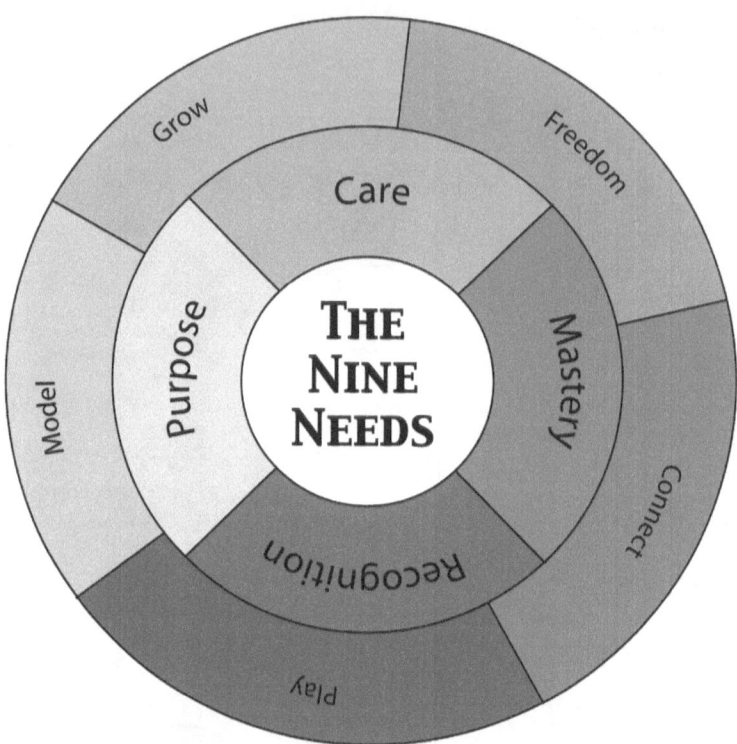

Minute 7: How do I make my team more cohesive this week, creating greater social bonding between members?

Minute 8: Where can I inject some fun this week?

Minute 9: What model do my employees need from me this week? Managers routinely model certain attitudes or behaviors, but sometimes the situation calls for something different or for special attention to some behavior. This question prods you to ponder the possibilities.

Of Robbins' nine topics, I think autonomy is the most important because it can have the biggest effect on a company's success.

Chapter 27 Hardest Thing in Business

We choose to go to the moon in this decade and do the other things, not because they are easy, but because they are hard.

~ John F. Kennedy, *Rice University Moon Speech (1962)*

There are many hard things to do in business. It takes wisdom to know what they are. It takes courage to choose to do them. The survival of a business depends on doing them.

Choosing priorities is the most difficult thing in business, specifically, choosing non-priorities. Non-priorities are the things you wish you could do, but cannot because you have better opportunities.

A common mistake leadership makes is to jump from crisis to crisis and tell their staff what the top priorities are, without looking at where the resources are going to come from and what that means won't get done on time, or at all. Often, senior managers are too busy to understand the side-effects of fixing the "big problem of the day".

Not understanding those impacts is very dangerous.

What these managers are doing is simply identifying things which are important. Anyone can do this. It is not good management. What is needed is *choosing* between things to do. This is the hard work.

> The hardest thing to do in business is not identifying priorities;
> it is choosing the non-priority to sacrifice.
> Any fool can identify priorities.

Everyone knows that resources are limited, but so often direct reports will accept the direction from senior management to make something top priority, without voicing concern over the impact on other important work. This may be due to the assumption that management understands these impacts and accepts the risk.

This is aggravated by managers thinking they understand the impact when they really do not. It may be worsened when staff cannot, on the spur of the moment, articulate all of the other work load and what will be impacted. It is very hard for any employee to quickly summarize all of their work in terms that can be understood and appreciated by a senior manager who is not really familiar with the work. Often, when a subordinate is trying to explain the work in dumbed-down terms, it sounds like less than it is, or worse, like an exaggeration or excuse.

Leadership must understand this axiom:

Every choice to do one thing is a choice to not do another thing.

It is the senior manager's duty to fully understand what is consuming the organization's capacity and how resources are being used.

Do, or do not, there is no try. -Yoda
Choose

Chapter 28 Avoiding Dumb Things

Ideas abound if you know where to look for them.

~ Neil Smith

How Excellent Companies Avoid Dumb Things

Neil Smith has written a good book titled, *How Excellent Companies Avoid Dumb Things,* about how to make change happen. It's not about the big ideas like *The Advantage* or *Great by Choice.* It is about the nitty gritty of getting change done. He explains that there are two things every company has:

– Hidden barriers that prevent great ideas from surfacing

– Employees with great ideas for how the company can do things differently

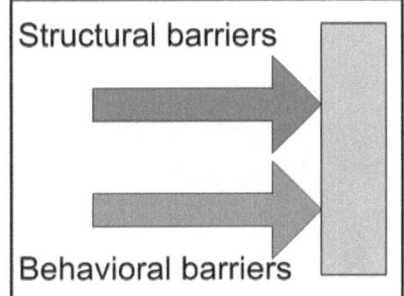

There are potentially thousands of ideas within your company. If unleashed, the impact of this could be dramatic:

- 25% increase in profit
- Less complexity
- Increased customer satisfaction

Eight Barriers to Great Ideas

1. Avoiding controversy
2. Poor use of time
3. Reluctance to change
4. Organizational silos
5. Management blockers
6. Incorrect information and bad assumptions
7. Size matters
8. Existing processes

Twelve Principles

There are twelve principles for breaking down these eight barriers:

1. The process must be personally led by the CEO and supported by senior management.

2. The entire organization must be engaged (not merely involved) in the change process.

3. The process is guided by a sprinkling of superstars from within the organization who are willing to challenge the status quo.

4. There are no predefined, finite or upfront targets for the company as a whole or for individual groups within it.

5. The ideas must be owned by the people responsible for implementing them

6. It must be easy to put ideas into the process for consideration, but hard to remove them.

7. The consideration of ideas is based on facts and analysis, not opinion.

8. Consensus is built so that everyone who will be affected by a change must agree with it before it is made. (This is the real secret to removing barriers.) See the inset on Goldratt's thinking processes on the next page.

9. There must be a focus on increasing revenue, not only on reducing expenses.

10. The process of breaking down the barriers may not disrupt normal business.

11. Anything less than 100% implementation is not acceptable.

12. The change process is about culture change; this is not simply a matter of completing a project.

Point number seven is pivotal. Ideas are given fair consideration without regard to who talks the loudest or cites a sample size of one. This is the essence of fact based decision making. This needs to become part of your culture. No one should be able to make claims without proof.

A Really Dumb Thing

Neal Smith illustrates this phenomena with a great story of a company which wanted to eliminate postage and paper use by offering emailed statements to customers who opted in for paperless statements. Because the IT department was too busy to do the job right, they added the ability to get emailed statements and when customers opted in, they would change their mailing address to be the company address. The statements would then get mailed as usual, then destroyed when they arrived at the mailroom, thereby incurring more cost. The IT department had provided the function, but not the benefit.

The Goldratt Thinking Processes

The *Thinking Processes* are a set of tools to help managers walk through the steps of initiating and implementing a project. When used in a logical flow, the *Thinking Processes* help walk through a buy-in process:

1. Gain agreement on the problem

2. Gain agreement on the direction for a solution

3. Gain agreement that the solution solves the problem

4. Agree to overcome any potential negative ramifications

5. Agree to overcome any obstacles to implementation

TOC practitioners sometimes refer to these in the negative as working through layers of resistance to a change.

Management as Referee

With senior management acting as referee, no one gets to bully their way to promote or kill an idea. The senior manager as referee is missing in most organizations.

Accountability is key. Senior management must be very attentive to keeping people from circumventing the process and killing good ideas they disagree with. The best way to do this is to *publically call people out when they demonstrate bad behavior*. Set the expectation that clever political maneuvering will not be tolerated. If necessary, fire a repeat offender to ensure that people know you are serious about making change happen.

Ideally, people who wish to make an argument based on talking the loudest or applying false logic should be in constant fear that they will be called out for this unwanted behavior.

If senior management sets the pattern of refereeing, and also the expectation that others should be doing the same in their absence, then making healthy decisions becomes the norm.

Chapter 29 Professional Business Travel

Why would you expect newly hired, recent college graduates to know how to do business travel? They don't teach it in school.

This is a note I wrote to another manager many years ago in reaction to some of my younger colleagues' mistakes. It won't exactly fit your circumstances, but you'll get the sense of it:

Frank,

You know Sean's work habits much better than I so I will leave it to you to provide him guidance.

I was disappointed lately with some of my junior staffers concerning their expectations for field installation trips. I found it necessary to explain that this is business travel, not tourism, even if it is to an interesting destination. We can, of course, arrange for people to take advantage of the destination after all of the work is done.

Here is some specific guidance:

- Safety is more important than anything

- We may not come home when we expect to

- Bring more sets of clothes than days planned

- You can't have too many tools with you

- Expect long days, and nights, seven days a week

- Expect delays in getting to eat hot, sit down meals

- If you whine about anything, no one will want to work with you

- Get yourself up in the morning and to the appointed rendezvous point promptly. No one is going to tell you when to wake up or eat breakfast.

- Plan to have your mobile phone charged and on 24 hours a day

- Do not plan to spend time making major purchases, visiting relatives, or knock off work early to catch a TV program

- Don't wash clothes yourself when you could be sleeping or working (we pay launderers to do it.)

- Check out of the hotel on the last day and do not leave bags in the room

- Get and keep receipts for everything

- Safety is more important than anything (sic)

California is warm and sunny, but San Francisco Bay is freakin' cold and windy even during the day. Be prepared for the unexpected.

The Air in Air Travel

The air on a jet is disgusting. To save on the cost of heating the cabin air from -40 degrees (no scale needed here; it's the same in F or C), airlines bring in very little fresh air. The air is full of germs and stink. So don't add your own. If there is a chance you will cough or sneeze, bring a handkerchief. Heck, bring a towel. Don't put your fingers in front of your face and pretend that you are catching all of your germs.

Also, please don't wear perfume or cologne and don't eat three-bean salad and drink stink-beer beforehand. Don't open a bag of beef jerky. Don't change a diaper at your seat.

Be a Gentle Traveler

I am writing this at 30,000 feet because it has happened again. The buffoon in front of me slammed his seat back like I was not even here.

I once had the person in front of me recline their seat so fast that the tray table catch shoved my laptop into my stomach. If you are going to recline your seat, be considerate of the person behind you. They may have their knee against the back of your seat, may be resting their head on the tray table, may have a full drink, or have a laptop on the tray.

Here's a better idea for reclining: don't. Let's admit that no one likes it when the seat in front of them leans back into their space. It always

Charlie Mitchell

makes us at least a little sad. So why would you do it to the person behind you? It is selfish. At least ask the person behind you if it's okay. If you can't do that, then at least warn them. You wouldn't do anything like that to people at home or work, so why do it just because there is a button in the armrest?

Feel free to move about the cabin, but...

Airplane seats are not rigid. The airlines make them as lightweight as they can. If you push on them, they move. If they move, so does the person sitting in it.

Even arching your back with just your head and feet touching, tips the seat way back. So don't plop yourself down like you are falling into your couch at home.

And don't yank on my seat back as you get in the row behind me. By all means, steady yourself, but avoid jarring other people. It's horrible to be jarred awake from airplane sleep.

I'm not done yet...

Be friendly, but don't assume that I want to hear your whole life story. If you do find someone who wants to talk, talk quietly; no one else wants to hear your amazing tales of last night.

Speaking of indecency, don't watch R-rated movies where kids and others can see them. Feel free to be ashamed in public.

Also, don't slam the overhead compartment shut. Yes, stewardess on the flight from Chicago, you too.

You know the rest, right?

- Cutting in line, pretending you don't see me

- Boarding before your turn

- Bringing a huge carry-on

- Selfishly sitting in the wrong seat on purpose (causing a lot of anxiety to another person who immediately starts to wonder if they won't have a seat)

- Trying to leave a bag that won't fit in the overhead compartment down by your feet hoping the stewardess won't see it

- Leaning on the person next to you
- Hanging parts of your body way into the aisle
- Playing loud music
- Taking your socks off
- Putting your feet up on the seat or arm-rest
- Putting your knees on the seat in front of you

Have some respect for the people sitting next to you and for the person behind you and in front of you. It's a lot of people in a really small space. Move gently.

How about at the airport terminal itself?

- Don't suddenly stop walking and stand in the way of everyone
- Don't stop at the end of the escalator or moving walkway
- Clean up your own garbage
- At the gate, if your zone has not been called, don't block the way of people who should be boarding

There, now I feel better.

Let's admit that no one likes it when the seat in front of them leans back into their space. It always makes us a little sad.
So why would you do it to the person behind you?

Chapter 30 Abundance Thinking

Focus on making more pie, not getting the most pie.

It's Not a Zero Sum Universe

People tend to fall into one of two camps. There are those who believe that in order for them to get more, someone else has to get less. This is called Zero-Sum thinking. It presumes that there is a finite amount of stuff to be had (food, money, power, happiness).

Then there are those who believe that there is no limit to how much stuff can be created, and the way to get more is to create more for everyone to share. Dave Thomas says it well: *Give everyone a chance to have a piece of the pie. If the pie's not big enough, make a bigger pie.*

This is our fear, but our daily reality is different. The truth is, there is plenty to go around. People need to stop hoarding it.

♦ ♦ ♦ ♦ ♦

Covey on Lose-Win and Win-Lose

Most of us learn to base our self-worth on comparisons and competition. We think about succeeding in terms of someone else failing--that is, if I win, you lose; or if you win, I lose. Life becomes a zero-sum game. There is only so much pie to go around, and if you get a big piece, there is less for me; it's not fair, and I'm going to make sure you don't get anymore. We all play the game, but how much fun is it really? ~ Stephen R. Covey

♦ ♦ ♦ ♦ ♦

Nothing makes you feel as rich as giving something away to another person who can really use it.

Malcolm Gladwell on Wealth

Here is an interesting concept: *The happiest people are the ones with a moderate amount of wealth.* In Malcolm Gladwell's, *David and Goliath*, he writes about the difficulty wealth causes to good parenting. He describes an inverted U-curve where ease of parenting increases with family income up to a maximum of $75k and then starts to get harder beyond that point.

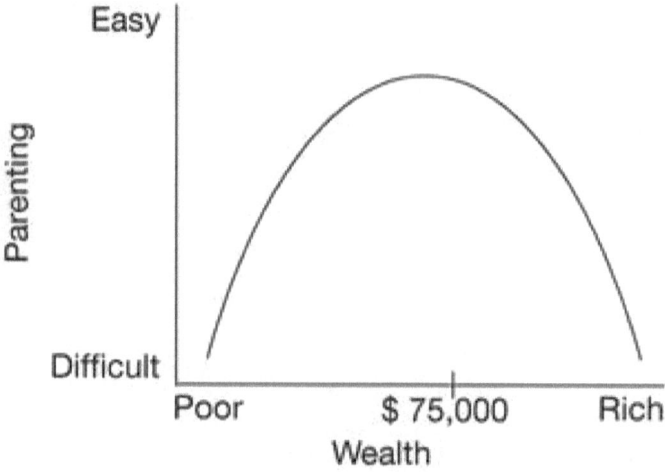

Chapter 31 Business Antipatterns

If you attempt to keep your business at its current size, it will die.

If it is not growing, it is dying.

~ Woody Levitan, *2005*

Collision Course

An antipattern is advice or a solution which looks (at first) like it may work, but is actually the opposite of what is needed.

C.S. Lewis describes a letter he got from a reader of *The Screwtape Letters* (the fictional correspondence between two satanic demons concerning advice on how to divert a faithful believer to hell), in which she said that she did not care very much for his book and that some of the advice given in it seemed almost diabolical. She did not get the joke at all.

Guidelines to Run Your Business into the Ground:

These are obvious ones to give you the hang of it.

Reputation

Go ahead and be dishonest. If you get caught, people will soon forget about it and want to do business with you again.

Teamwork

Make your employees compete with each other rather than work together. It is more fun to watch, and that is the point of running a business, right, to be entertained watching underlings scratch out a living?

Risk

Try to avoid all risks. Pass up on contracts with risk. Price bids high enough to cover all possible risks.

People

Hire the cheapest people willing to do the work. You can always hire more quality control personnel later to catch all the defects.

Planning

No one can predict the future, so do not waste time trying. Budgets and forecasts are pointless.

Staffing Levels

Hire fewer people than you need to do the job right. You will make more money this way and your people will be thrilled to help work on bids and proposals which will bring them more work to do. Staff who are hungry for new work do not write the best proposals; it is people who are drowning in work who will gladly take more time away from their families to win more projects.

Poka-Yoke

Do not waste resources creating mechanisms for preventing people from making mistakes. Leave hazardous and unclear situations alone. No one will learn the hard way if error is designed out of the process. The company can afford to deal with the same breakage over and over.

Do these and you will be out of business in no time.

◆ ◆ ◆ ◆ ◆

Good Idea?

A billion dollar company for which I did consulting decided that they would mitigate the risk of outsourced software development. They originally got a bid from vendor A who would use Vendor B as a sub-contractor.

Rather than keep that simple approach, the company decided to contract directly with both vendors, splitting the work between them and adding a clause in their contracts which said that at any time, the company could transfer work from one vendor to the other. The thought was that if vendor A got behind schedule or could not provide enough labor resources, the work could just be reassigned.

At the surface, this seemed like a clever solution to lower risk, but it was not.

First, the total of the two bids was twenty percent higher than the bid from a single prime contractor using the other vendor as a subcontractor.

Next, this now put the company in the role of acting as the arbiter every time one vendor was dependent on the other for pre-requisite work. Neither vendor had contractual leverage to compel the other to prioritize work correctly.

There were now three design authorities competing to make technical decisions. The resulting debates slowed the design process way down.

Each vendor was motivated to make the other vendor fail so they would get more of the contract.

This approach might work well for repetitive manufacturing or a service like printing, but it was a recipe for disaster for a complex software system design/build project.

You need to know when good sounding advice is actually bad advice. Those are antipatterns.

Chapter 32 Authority and Accountability

You can't stop a teacher when they want to do something.
They just do it.

~ J.D. Salinger, *The Catcher in the Rye (1945)*

Taken, Not Given

Early in one's career, it is easy to wish for authority. It is common to imagine that authority means having the liberty of making decisions without having to justify the need, or own the outcome. Neither is true.

To begin with, authority is never given, it can only be taken. You have to exercise authority. You can do so in proportion to the responsibility you have been given, and surprisingly, to the degree of trust you have from your peers. You may find yourself in the difficult position of having responsibility to do something, but not having enough trust from those over whom you attempt to exercise authority to get them to act. This is a sign of an ineffectual leader.

> Authority is never given, it can only be taken.

People will question your authority. At B&K I was project manager for a systems integration project. This was a company that did not normally do turnkey systems so there were no established methods. I wrote up a purchase order, signed my own name, and took it to purchasing. The head of purchasing asked where I got my authority to sign. I simply said I was responsible for delivering the $648k system and these were things I needed to do the job.

I did not make the mistake of undermining myself by citing the authority of my boss or someone more senior. I cited the job I was responsible for as my source of legitimacy.

Interestingly, years later I was working on an $849K project at TRMI and at the project kickoff meeting, our purchasing agent asked the General Manager what my level of authority for purchase orders would be. The GM said, "For the whole thing," to which the purchasing guy responded, "Yes, but what is the maximum size PO for Charlie's signature?" The GM responded, "You don't get it. Up to $849k on a single PO if that's what Charlie wants."

The Triad

In a properly functioning organization, authority, responsibility, and accountability are all connected. When someone makes you responsible for something, it is then incumbent on you to exercise the authority needed to fulfill that responsibility.

Unlike authority, responsibility *can* be given, but cannot be shed. When delegating, if you make someone responsible for doing something, you are still responsible to your superiors to ensure that the task gets done. This does not mean that you are to do it. In fact, that would be very bad delegation. You are responsible to follow-up at agreed upon intervals, and ensure the work is being done correctly.

> Unlike authority, responsibility *can* be given.
> Responsibility cannot be shed.

This mechanism is called accountability. It is imperative that the delegator make the goal well understood, make it clear how often they will check in, and then follow-up exactly as promised. If you fail to check in along the way as agreed, and the task does not get done, that is your failure. You cannot hold someone accountable for vague requests, nor when you failed to get status updates that would give you early warning about the need to intervene.

Reliable Promises and Commitments

How do we get good commitments from people that we can hold them to? In most organizations, if you have a simple excuse like, I had too much else to do, you can duck responsibility for getting your assignment done.

When you ask people why they failed to meet a commitment, you are training them to look for, and give, excuses for failure. Instead, simply state your dissatisfaction with the fact that their last commitment was not reliable and ask them when they can be relied upon to finish. Do not be unduly harsh, but remember that being overly gracious and empathetic encourages a low-performing culture.

Hal Macomber has a great approach in his *Promising Poster* where he talks about getting the promisor to make a commitment based on five key elements:

- Having the necessary competence
- Having understood the time required
- Blocking out the time needed
- Freely making the promise
- Be responsible for any upset that occurs from failing

These need to be done with clarity about what is being promised (scope) and when it is to be done (schedule).

Hal Macomber's Promising Poster:

Five Basic Elements of a Promise	Five Elements of a Reliable Promise
Speaker (performer) – This is you. Be clear that you are making the commitment, not someone else.	I am **competent** (able) to perform the task and have the wherewithal or I have access to both with the help of others.
Listener (customer) – This is the customer or someone depending on your performance. He or she already made a request.	I understand or **have estimated how much time** it will take me to perform this task.
Mutually understood Conditions of Satis-faction – Many breakdowns occur due to a misunderstanding of what is being requested. What is obvious to one is not obvious to the other, particularly when people may have just met each other.	I have (already) **blocked out time in my calendar** that I need to perform the task.
Future action – When we make a promise, we are saying that sometime in the future (before the due date) we will perform some action to bring about the designed outcome or condition of satisfaction.	**I am freely making this promise.** I am not having a private, unspoken conversation to the contrary.
Due date – This is the second source of miscoordination. One person thinking "now" while the other person is thinking "when I get around to it." Always err on the side of explicitly specifying the required date.	I know that when I make a promise I may not be able to fulfill it. **I will be responsible for any upset that occurs should I not be able to perform the task**, including any negative consequences that may come my way.

Credit: Hal Macomber

Chapter 33 Status Updates from Your Team

If you know the right thing to do, do it now.

How do your people update you on their work?

Assessing the evolution of your role in managing people is a complex matter, but one useful aspect is how your direct reports provide you with updates on how their assignments are progressing.

There are four types of updates your direct reports might provide to you:

I have a problem. What should I do?

I have a problem. Here's what I'm thinking. What's your experience?

I have a problem. Here's what I'm doing. Stop me if I am wrong.

I had a problem. Here's what I did. I just wanted you to know.

What types of updates are your people currently giving you? Are you clear about the kind of updates you expect and under what circumstances you expect them? You need to be very specific in order to get the result you want.

When you are specific about responsibility in terms of the level of decision making authority people have, and how and when they should seek guidance, you will get another benefit in addition to them giving you updates the way you want. They will make decisions faster. Faster decisions improve business velocity, which directly affects profitability.

Just make sure you have provided the simple and clear *Commander's Intent* so your people can achieve the right objective.

> Faster decisions improve business velocity,
> which directly affects profitability.

Chapter 34 Right Seat on the Submarine

Get the right people on the submarine

Get the wrong people off the submarine.

Get the right people in the right seat on the submarine.

The Bus Analogy Breaks Down

The expression "get the right people on the bus" is part of this set:

- Get the right people on the bus

- Get the wrong people off of the bus

- Get everyone into the right seat on the bus

And since most organizations struggle with the first two, little attention is paid to the third tenant.

The third tenant is where the analogy breaks down. Beside the driver's seat on a bus, all of the seats are essentially the same. The analogy succeeds in communicating the notion of traveling together. It communicates the sense of having a unified destination equally well. The bus is a single container.

And since, according to Jim Collins, author of the books "Good To Great" and "Great by Choice", you want people to choose to get on the bus not because of where it is going, but because of who else is getting on the bus, the concept of having the right team is reinforced and the focus is on who is on the team and who is not on the team.

The weakness of the analogy is the seats on the bus themselves. All of the seats except for the one the driver occupies are comparable. On a bus, the seats are window or aisle, front or rear, but all serve the same function. Any passenger can sit in any seat. This is not how companies work.

In a reality, job roles are normally very different. This makes one big difference between a bus and submarine. On a submarine, "seat" is highly specialized and the crew members are not interchangeable. The sonar guy does the sonar, the helmsman steers etc. So if the cook is a bad cook, the food is bad, no one else can cook because that seat is taken. Everyone suffers with bad food.

> In a dysfunctional organization, when someone is bad
> at their job, other people sneak in and do the work
> without them or re-work their output.
> This is a terrible approach that perpetuates the
> low performance and drives up cost.

As managers, we often focus on the issue that employee is not performing well, may not be satisfied, may be delivering late, or have low quality output. But there is another problem.

As long as an underperformer is in a given seat, and that seat is not made vacant, and the organization will not hire another person to do that job. The role is blocked by the current occupant. This problem is worse in small organizations than large ones where it is easier to create a new, similar role.

It really matters what role someone has within the organization. Even the best and brightest will underperform in the wrong role, but worse they keep the company from putting the right person in that role. A company is more like a submarine than a bus.

Too often, the only choices that are seen with an employee is "on or off the bus". And often they are not so horrible at the role they have that you want to fire them. But as long as they are in that seat, no one else can be in that seat and do the job the way it needs to be done.

The challenge to a good manager is to move the person from the wrong seat and free up the role for someone who can do it correctly.

Part 6 – Project Management

Time is not a resource. Why? Because you cannot control the rate at which it is expended. It goes by one hour per hour no matter what else we do to manage a project.

~ John Storck, *Project Management Guru*

Chapter 35 Real Project Management

Find the three things on a project that are going to turn to mush and pay attention to those. The rest will get done.

~ Jim Talley

A Micro-rant about PERT and CPM

I believe that MS-Project has done the profession of project management a great disservice, since anyone who can draw a Gantt chart with MS-Project can be deluded into thinking they understand project management. Many only look at the planning aspect and forget control completely.

MS-Project is an amazingly powerful tool for project planning and control and yet nearly every MPP file cannot calculate the critical path correctly.

Go to your last MPP. Select the network view (now harder to find than ever on new versions). Chances are it will look like this - with one or more tasks which are not the predecessor to anything.

(You don't need to read the characters on this chart because they don't matter. Just notice the unconnected task.)

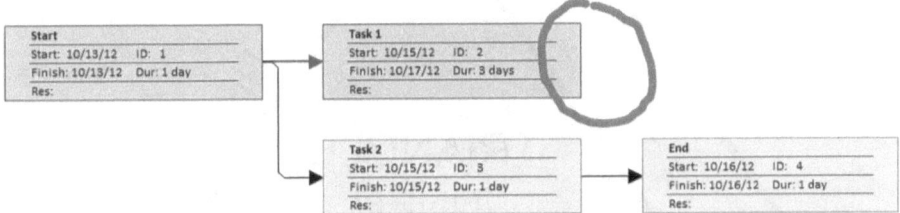

So in theory, you don't need to do Task-1 to complete the project.

If Task-1 has no dependent task, why do it at all? According to this chart, there is nothing dependent on Task-1. In reality, at a minimum, the last milestone is dependent on it. But without this connection, you can't calculate the critical path correctly.

This is a result of people thinking that if they can master the software, well enough to draw a Gantt chart, they can practice the science. But if you don't know how to go from WBS to CPM by hand, the software won't help you do anything but generate form without substance.

◆ ◆ ◆ ◆ ◆

I had a client ask me to remove the vertical lines connecting task finishes to task starts in MS-Project. I thought he wanted the lines to no longer display. No, he wanted the predecessor relationships removed! He just wanted to use it as a drawing tool.

MS-Project is not just a drawing tool!

◆ ◆ ◆ ◆ ◆

A project may be viewed as a pair of concentric triangles where the sides represent time, resource and technical objective.

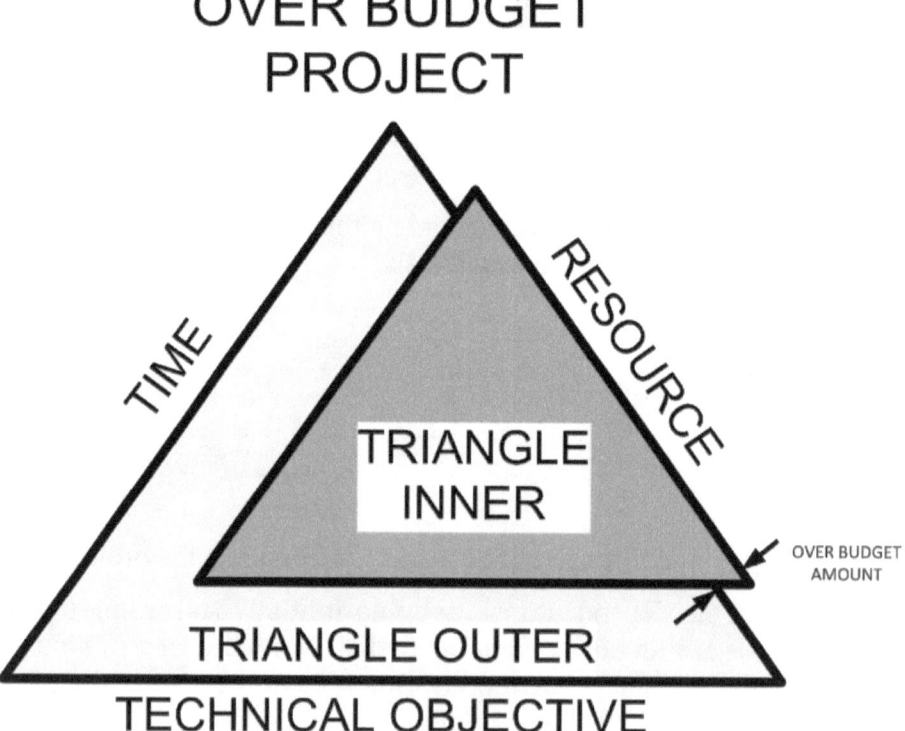

Triangle inner *must stay within triangle* outer *to stay on plan.*

– John Storck

Managing schedule is critical to managing scope. The best way to bring a project in on-budget is to complete it quickly. Delays bring the risk of scope creep with this vicious cycle:

The Vicious Cancer

The longer a project takes, the more it costs

The more it costs, the longer it takes

The longer it takes, the more opportunities exist to change scope

The more changes in scope, the more it costs

The more it costs, the longer it takes

At one time, I was working on a system integration project proposal for a large corporation and I had provided a professional scheduler some task durations as working days and others, like a 90-day operational test in elapsed-days (i.e., calendar days). When I saw the plan, the 90 elapsed day task had been reduced to 66 working days. When I pointed out the error, I was told that they don't use elapsed days. But 66 working days was only 88 elapsed days.

"Oh," I was told, "We assume 22 working days per month."

"But 90 days is not three months," I explained. "Months are different sizes. This test is supposed to be exactly 90 days long. The customer doesn't want to see a 90-day test last only 88 days."

"Oh, we can adjust it to 68 days."

"What about when the start date changes and the weekends (non-working days) change?"

"We'll change it by hand each time." (So much for automation)

Concrete takes four days to cure to usable strength.
It does not take the weekend off.

Chapter 36 Critical Chain Project Management

*The Critical Chain does away with milestones, multitasking
and per-activity contingency time and advocates project
contingency buffers and a roadrunner mentality instead.*

~ Peter Schneider-Kamp *(June 13, 2002)*

Why This Matters

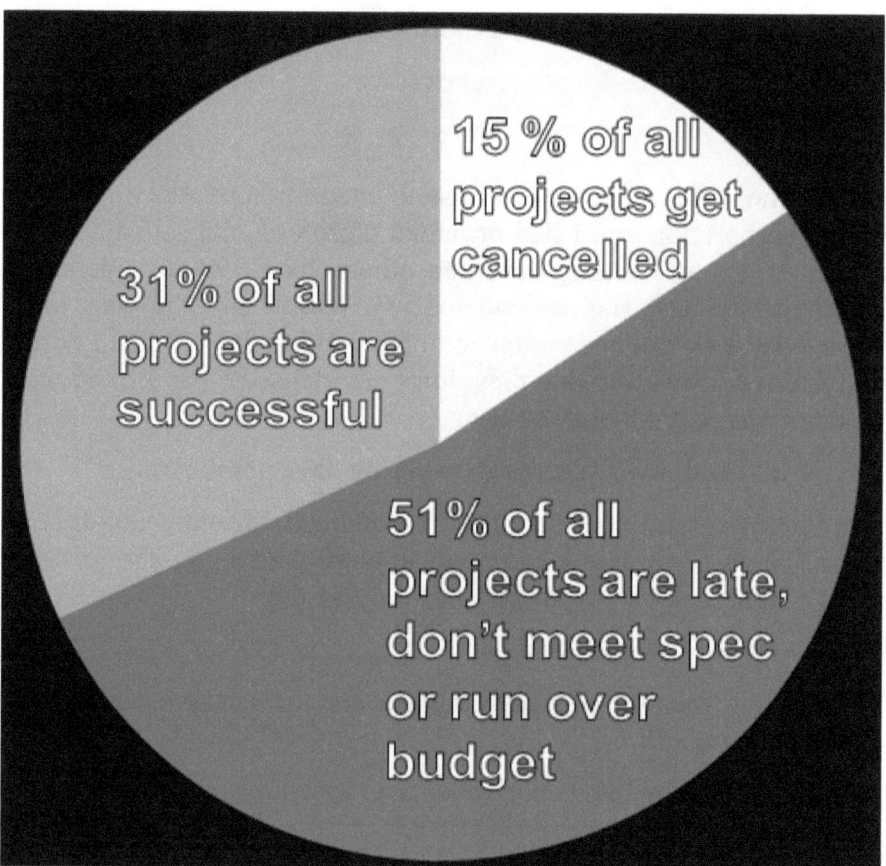

Can you imagine if bank transactions, car production or hospital surgeries had these numbers? No one would accept it.

Applying the Theory of Constraints

Eli Goldratt first wrote about the application of his theory of constraints to manufacturing operations in his seminal book, *The Goal*. He has also applied it to project management work in his book, *The Critical Chain* giving birth to Critical Chain Project Management.

Theory of constraints is based on the premise that the rate of goal achievement by a goal-oriented system (i.e., the system's throughput) is limited by at least one constraint. A constraint is a bottleneck or choke point. Only by increasing flow through that constraint can over-all throughput be increased. This is the basis of CCPM.

Buffer Time

The critical chain takes chaos into consideration and looks at how contingency (time buffers) eat up schedule. Critical chain project management treats time buffers differently by sparingly applying time buffers to sub-critical paths to allow for chaos to prevent them from becoming the critical path as a surprise. Specifically, time buffers are placed in front of constraints to prevent them from ever starving for input.

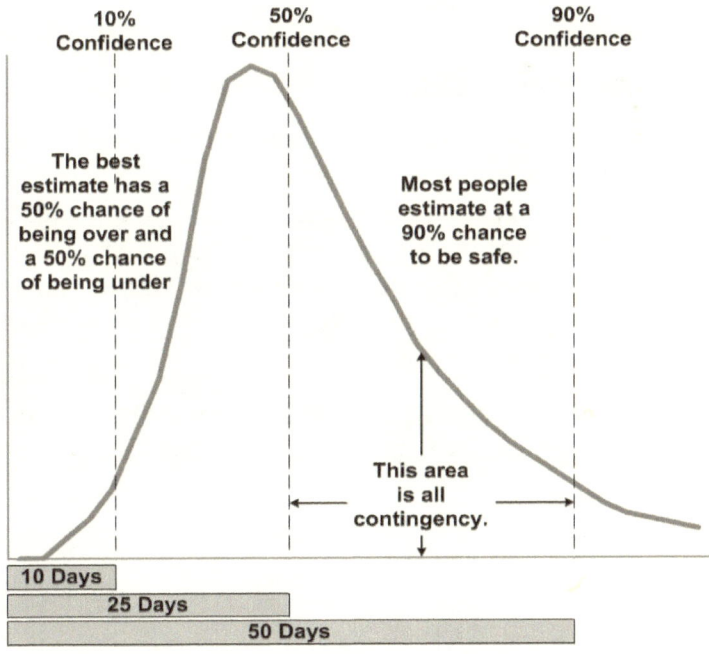

How People Estimate

Most people estimate with a 90% chance of completing on or before the estimated completion time. They are not being dishonest. They are compensating for expected delays based on experience. No one wants to be late 50% of the time.

So Why Still Late?

With that much slack or contingency, why are tasks still late so frequently? There are at least three reasons:

1. Parkinson's Law - Actually, a corollary to Parkinson's law about group size. The work expands to fill the available time. If people see that they are going to finish before the time is up, they embellish or do non-essential re-work. This is the opposite of the minimally marketable feature set concept found in agile software development.

2. Student Syndrome - A commonly observed human behavior is to combine these flaws which create last minute work:

- Failure to correctly size work (*more work than anticipated*)

- Failure to perceive chaos events (*unexpected delays*)

- Failure to defer gratification (*causes late start*)

3. Due Date Focus - This is an organizational, not individual defect. The requirement placed on people is to complete their work by the date due. This can be so ingrained that people can't see the problem with it. Can you? Focusing on the due date invites late starts caused by other tasks and interruptions. If you plan to complete on the last possible date, *only if nothing else goes wrong* will the task get done when it should.

People who plan on the latest possible start are betting on no chaos, completely ignoring their own experience with delays.

Process and Approach

Critical Chain project management requires us to collect the buffer time built into individual estimates and manage it as one resource pool:

- Get the 50 and 90% estimates
- Separate the probable time from the safe time
- Aggregate the safe time and move it to the end of the project
- Focus on finishing as early as possible
- Focus on the team as a whole finishing the project – late is a team issue
- Monitor the use of buffer time, not task progress (earned value is of dubious value, except in software where it is useless.)
- Prioritize resources based on buffer use, not project importance

Practice

Assuming the goal of a system has been articulated and its measurements defined, the steps are:

1. Identify the system's constraint(s) (that which prevents the organization from obtaining more of the goal in a unit of time)
2. Decide how to exploit the system's constraint(s) (how to get the most out of the constraint)
3. Subordinate everything else to the above decision (align the whole system to support the decision made above)
4. Elevate the system's constraint(s) (make other major changes needed to increase the constraint's capacity)
5. Warning! If in the previous steps, a constraint has been broken, go back to step 1, but do not allow inertia to cause a system constraint.

The goal of a commercial organization is: *Make more money now and in the future*, and its measurements are given by throughput accounting as: throughput, inventory, and operating expenses.

> *Even brief mental blocks created by shifting between tasks can cost as much as 40 percent of someone's productive time.* – David Meyer

The Hidden Cost of Multitasking

Multitasking isn't. No one really does two things at once. Studies have shown that multitasking can be very bad for knowledge worker productivity because of the time cost of context switching. For intensive work like software programming, any attention diverted to a momentary minor distraction like an email notification on screen, even if it goes unread, can lead to losing place mentally. It can take minutes to recover from getting a cup of coffee.

Likewise, multitasking on a project is switching between tasks and it has a bad effect on completion dates. Because multitasking delays any single task from being completed *As-soon-as-possible*, the actual completion can be significantly later than the *Earliest-Possible-Finish* had the task been dwelled upon until it was finished.

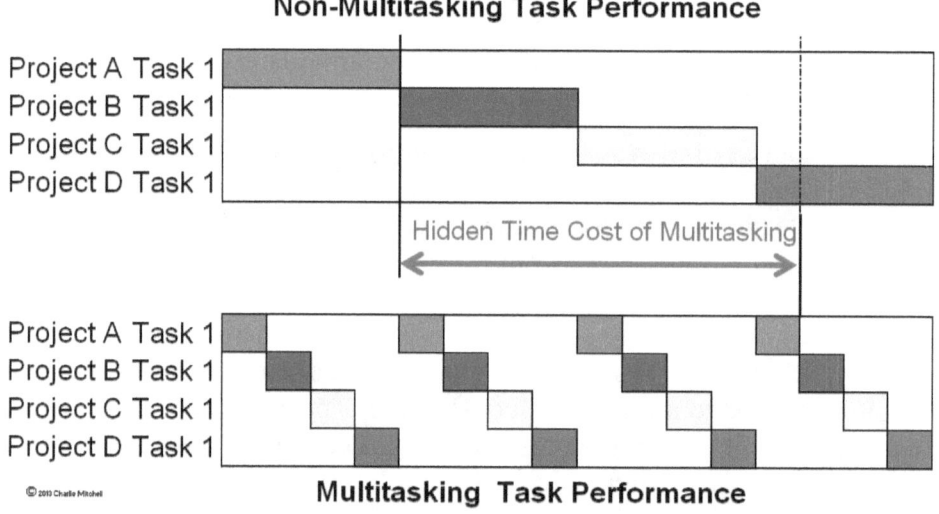

Non-Multitasking Task Performance

Hidden Time Cost of Multitasking

Multitasking Task Performance

With multitasking, most dependent tasks are delayed from starting until later than necessary. Compare the completion date of the two green Project A tasks to see the hidden time cost of multitasking.

Chapter 37 Estimating

Who wants to be consistently wrong fifty percent of the time?

~ Joe Ely, *2001*

Storck's Five Rules of Estimating

From John C. Storck, JR, Storck Associates American Management Association:

1. The best estimate has the highest probability of being realized during execution (neither under nor over). The estimate should have a 50% chance of being under and a 50% chance of being over. It should contain neither padding nor contingency. It is not a guaranteed completion date. Contingency should be added by the PM who can then aggregate and move around slack.

2. Estimates should be supplied by the persons who will perform the work. This is because they are most familiar with the task, but more importantly it forms a contract-like commitment to execute the work as planned.

3. Estimates should be rendered at an appropriate level of WBS detail. Overall size, risk and urgency (distance from the critical path) determine how far down the work breakdown schedule estimating should be done.

4. Estimates should account for time/cost/resource tradeoffs. Economies of scale, waste, yield, capacity, and efficiency can all be used to influence the duration and cost of a task. If less time can be spent by using more of a given resource, this should be considered.

5. Productivity should be an estimate factor. Actual, not theoretical productivity should be used. Allowances for normal, non-producing activities such as time lost to context switches, un-assigned or un-documented tasks, travel, and personal business should be included in the estimate. Other factors such as working conditions, equipment availability, tool conditions, distance, and weather affect productivity.

Scope

The quality of an estimate is directly proportionate to the quality of the statement of work being requested. An incomplete scope of work will lead to underestimating. This is a common problem when non-technical people ask engineers for estimates.

Potential changes in scope should not be considered in an estimate (but should always be brought to the PM's attention).

However, unknown problems, which cannot be identified, but are common occurrences, can be included in the scope for estimating purposes (e.g., we do not know which boards need to be replaced until we remove the cover, but typically 15% need replacing; or we do not know what unknown bugs the software will have, but usually we spend 20% more time for debugging).

Recalibrating

By making estimates, documenting them, recording actual expenditures and comparing, it is possible to improve estimating. A PM should always be advised when an estimator has changed methods so they know how to revise their contingency. There should be a lot of discussion about the meaning of an estimate when two people are working together for the first time.

Is That All There Is?

Years ago at PSC, after a few rounds of surprises, we developed *Charlie's Estimating Test*. At the completion of each round of estimating we would ask, *If we strictly did only the things on our estimate would that be everything we need or is there something else we would need?* Usually this would produce a few rounds of revisions until everyone was satisfied that we had everything included.

Chapter 38 Change Orders and Contingency

Contingency is the budget you have set aside to buy customer satisfaction or to avoid more expensive alternatives like litigation.

Every project budget should have an appropriate amount of contingency budget to pay for un-funded work that the customer wants. This is different from the customer's public change-order allowance in the contract. This is your private financial contingency cushion. Whatever portion of your contingency does not get spent becomes pure profit from the project. This private contingency should never be spent without receiving some gain for it.

Change Order Paper Trail

Rule 1 - Never tell the customer you have your own contingency budget.

Rule 2 - You should always submit a change order form, even if it is a zero dollar change order. The customer will just consider this to be good configuration management.

Rule 3 - There should be an email for every change and they should have a consistent subject line like this:

A. Project name (this should already be standard for everyone and every project email)

B. *Change Order*

C. (*Add, Increase, Extend, Extra, Additional, or More*) + (*Time, Parts, Hours, Functions*)

For example, *Website Project Change Order for Extra Pages*

Use the phrase "change order" consistently so if the customer searches their email (or if you have to later to make a case for a claim) there is a long list of emails with *change order* in the subject line.

Until you charge the customer, you are just doing good configuration/change management; they can't complain.

No-Charge Change Orders

Remember, your customer always KNOWS they are asking for extras; they only pretend they do not know.

When they do:

1. Ask casually if there is an RFP reference or drawing/print (there isn't)

2. Just say the cost out loud, dollars or hours etc.

3. Wait 7 seconds like you are figuring the impact on your budget (look up and left, slightly shake your head left-to-right)

4. Look him in the eye, nod and say, "We can do that for you." (Big relief to him, confrontation avoided.) If he thanks you, immediately say "You are welcome".

5. Tell him you'll send a follow-up email with the scope details

6. Say "When you see it, reply and let me know I have the scope details right."

7. Title the email as above

8. When he concurs, immediately send over a change management form for signature with $0 as the amount. Request acknowledgement.

9. When you are almost done being charitable, give him fair warning. Say, "We'll eat this one, but this is the last freebie." <u>Never surprise your customer</u>.

For-Fee Change Orders

When it's time to charge him:

1. Offer a lesser, unworkable solution, including not doing it. Ask, "Are you sure it's worth the investment?"

2. Say you can do the lesser item for free or some low-ball figure.

3. Wait for him to say it won't work.

4. Say you'll have to think on it and see if there is any way to avoid the cost of what he wants.

5. Follow up with an email (same subject line approach as above) with the price in the body of the email.

6. Ask him if you have the details (scope) right, don't ask about the price.

7. When he concurs, send over a change management form for signature.

8. If he balks, it won't be because he never got anything for free from you before. If you have followed the above process for work done out of your contingency budget several times, he KNOWS he has gone to the well enough times.

9. If he balks give him three choices:

   A. Find it in the RFP, specifications, or plans (it's still not there)

   B. The lessor solution (be careful, this can backfire, he may force you to make a bad solution work correctly)

   C. The for-fee change order

Project Delays

Customer induced project delays can be documented the same way. You don't always want to seek an extension for every little delay, but they add up and your project can die a death of a thousand cuts.

Send the customer an email with the word "Delay" in the subject line every time they are behind schedule with an approval, review, meeting, customer provided material, etc.

It does not need to be obnoxious like this: Website Project - Customer Created Schedule Delay of Three Weeks.

It can be subtle use of the word "delay", like this: Website Project - Ideas for Compensating for Delayed Access to Plant Engineering Staff, or Website Project - Rescheduling Delayed Review Meeting to Nov 19

This way, you are part of the solution.

But if you have to make a claim for time later, all the customer needs to do is search for *Delay* and up comes every email on the topic.

BONUS TOPIC

Injurious Subject Lines

If the customer sends you an email with a damning subject line like, "Website Project - Multiple Contractor Safety Infractions Onsite!!!" don't reply without *changing the subject line*.

In this case, change it to something like, "Website Project - Improving Onsite Contractor Safety."

There is no need to have dozens of emails with a bad subject line floating around.

It is <u>always</u> okay to improve subject lines.

Part 7 – Marketing and Sales

The only successful long-term marketing strategy is
to help your customer achieve their goals.

Chapter 39 Dependability

How do you get customers waiting in line to do business with you?

Be Dependable

Be dependable and the world will beat a path to your door. This is not complicated, it just takes some discipline.

Step 1. Staying in Touch

The timing of it is the trick. There are four periods:

1. Before the customer wonders how it is going

2. When the customers wishes you would call

3. When the customer is concerned that they have not heard

4. When too much time has passed and now it is awkward

I learned this from a part-time handyman who was very much in demand. His whole business strategy seemed to simply be to be dependable. He was so much in demand that he often booked work for six months ahead.

After people had signed up for work and given him a deposit, he knew that he would be on time, but he also understood that customers begin to get anxious beforehand. So he would call them a couple of months ahead of the start date and tell them he would be starting on time. Then a month later, he would tell them he was going to order materials. Then when the materials arrived, he would let them know they had arrived and he would be starting the exact day he said he would. Then, of course, he would show up on time. Since he always called before the customer got concerned, they stayed relaxed the whole time.

Step 2. Follow Through

Since he booked his work so thoughtfully, with schedule slack to accommodate the inevitable obstacles, he could complete the job without having to go away for a few days to handle some other customer with a broken commitment. Whatever slack he did not use, he would fill in with one-day jobs or work on his own income properties. By planning well and staying in touch, his customer satisfaction is much higher than the average general contractor.

Step 3. Deliver on Your Commitment

Do what you say you would, when you said you would. Your work could be the best quality in the world, but if you deliver it late, it is tainted with disappointment. For this reason, learning how to estimate timing well and learning how to tell customers the truth when it is not what they want to hear are two valuable skills.

Results

People refer work to my handyman friend constantly. He has no marketing costs; his reputation does it all for him. He simply is dependable by staying in touch, starting on time, and staying on the job until completion. For this kind of service, people often are willing to wait for him for over six months.

Chapter 40 Negotiating

*You will never make more money per hour
than when you are negotiating.*

~ Stephen W. Gibson

Quiz

Here is a collection of experts' sayings about negotiating. Some of this advice is suspect. Can you tell which ones are bad?

In a negotiation, he who cares less, wins. ~ Anonymous
Counter: *In a negotiation, he who prepares best and knows his own and his counterpart's situation best, wins.*

Never negotiate on a full stomach. ~ Victor Antonetti
Counter: *Unless you are negotiating for food.*

If you're planning on doing business with someone again, don't be too tough in the negotiations. If you're going to skin a cat, don't keep it as a house cat. ~ Marvin Levin
Corollary: *It's hard to predict when you will run into someone again. Always assume you are going to do business with someone again. It's always better to 'leave a little money on the table' than try to 'skin a cat.'*

If you don't like what you're hearing, respond with a question, even if it's no more than, 'Why are you saying that?' ~ Mark McCormack

Talk about price last. People have tremendous anxieties about hearing the price, so use preliminary negotiations to get all the auxiliary issues resolved first. Say, 'If the price is OK, would you be willing to...?' ~ Jay Kaplan

Round numbers beg to be negotiated, usually by counteroffer round numbers. Odd numbers sound harder, firmer, less negotiable. ~ Mark McCormack

Don't go into a negotiation without listing every issue beforehand. Establish an aspiration level, a minimum, and an initial asking price for each issue. ~ Charles Karrass

As a buyer approaching a negotiating meeting, be sure to trumpet any bad economic news headlines as much as possible. – Chip Conley

Successful negotiations are 70% preparation, 20% implementation, and 10% acting. ~ Robert Olson

Throw a temper tantrum within the first ten minutes of the negotiating – nine out of ten times it will effectively intimidate your opponent. ~ Mark Randall

If negotiations are a regular part of your business, make sure all your negotiators have been to Karrass training. The amount of anecdotal and just plain bad information about "how to negotiate" provided by supposed experts is staggering. – S. Milford (see example immediately above)

Be prepared to walk away. ~ Anonymous

Chapter 41 Oral Presentations

Customers are concerned with three things: me, me, and me.

~ Laverne Caceres, *President, The Professional Voice*

What Are You Selecting?

Imagine yourself as your customer at an oral presentation of your company's proposal.

What are you selecting?

You are selecting the team of people you are going to spend the next months working with. You are not selecting a stack of parts.

So you have to convince your customer that you are the kind of people they want to hire.

This means that the centerpiece of your presentation needs to be the project team, not the sales people, the management, product specialists, or the products.

This means that you need to carefully select the project team prior to submitting the proposal, based on how well they present, not just how well they fit the RFP qualification requirements.

If the first time your project manager meets your customer is at the oral presentation, you are starting from a hole.

> The customer is choosing people to work with for the next months or years. They want to pick people they will like working with.

Three Principles – Meaning, Benefit, Credibility

Each slide in a sales presentation must address these three aspects:

1. What's your point? (Meaning)

The listener needs to understand what you are saying, and why you are saying it. They need to be able to comprehend your meaning. Make your point clearly. If you don't, they may be thinking, so what? Who cares? Tell what to conclude.

> *Unfortunately, most speakers send audience members on what we call, 'journeys of self-discovery'. Most of the time we are just shipping you off…saying "Have a great time; there are all kinds of things you can discover."* ~ Douglas Jefferys

2. What's in it for me? (Benefit)

Do not leave your customer guessing about the benefit of what you are talking about. Tell them. Be explicit. If you are being scored, make sure you *answer the mail* in a way that makes it clear that your offering has a benefit to them. If you talk about how old and big your company is (I just described your first slide, didn't I?) without making it clear how they get value from it, then you are just bragging. If you can connect that company information to a benefit for them (e.g., risk reduction), then you have succeeded.

3. Prove it! (Credibility)

Once you have made a claim, you need to substantiate it somehow to make it credible. Not every proof has to be built on unimpeachable evidence, but every proof has to have a plausible connection to the truth. It may be enough to cite that someone else believes it. It can be as trivial as being specific about details and facts to demonstrate that your claim is real. Use numbers, percentages, dates, and names.

Chapter 42 Qualifying Opportunities

*Anyone can consume a sales team's time with
no cost to themselves.*

B.A.N.T.

Nothing is more wasteful than someone who ties up sales people and does not buy. A lot of salespeople want to put the maximum number of leads into the sales process that they can. They are thinking that it is a numbers game, with no skill involved. This is a bad combination that can squander an organization's resources if not held in check.

A good sales person will filter out all the unlikely prospects and focus on the real opportunities. The question is not, *Do we want this work?* but, *Can we win this bid?*

The methods for qualifying potential customers vary by industry and deal size. For big ticket sales, try to get the following information:

B budget

A authority

N need

T timeline

If a prospect does not have sufficient budget, authority or need, or if the deal is way off in the future, it is probably not worth actively putting substantial effort into it.

It may be that you want to cultivate relationships at this company slowly, but not incur a lot of expense doing elaborate demonstrations or executive visits. Instead, find something of value, like free consulting, to give them. This will allow you to invest work in other opportunities that have a higher probability of being won in the near term.

As a result, your win ratio will go up, and your cost of sales will go down - a double benefit.

Chapter 43 Are We Bidding or Not?

In a distributed organization, it is imperative that every-one knows what bid stage you are in.

The Bid/No-Bid Decision

It is very possible for a major bid and pricing effort to cost hundreds of thousands of dollars. If you knew in advance that you were going to lose, you would decide not to bid and that cost savings would go right to your bottom line. How much do you need to sell to make that much in profit?

Portrayed this way, it is easy to see how critical a bid/no-bid decision is. And if you think the answer is to put in a low quality, low budget proposal, you are just wasting money.

Some imprudent sales people will push to have all of their opportunities make it past the bid/no-bid decision. They need to be stopped.

Criteria

Your specific criteria will vary, but two trustworthy tests are:

- Can we win?

- Will it enhance our image?

Note that neither has anything to do with profit. That's because the people who make these decisions must both understand profit and the broader destiny of the company.

The Bid/No-Bid Presentation

It is very common to have a PowerPoint deck for bid/no-bid decision meetings. Here are some typical slides:

1. Title

2. Opportunity Overview

3. Opportunity Summary

4. RFP Schedule

5. High Level SOW

6. Sub-Systems

7. Competition

8. System Diagram

9. Preliminary Project Time Schedule

10. Proposed Teaming Structure

11. Price ROM

12. Terms and Conditions

13. Risks

14. Bid/No-bid Red Green

15. Recommendation

Whatever method you use, it should have rigorous and unambiguous criteria that make it easy for everyone to reach the same conclusion.

Are We Bidding or Not?

When a conclusion is reached, make sure everyone understands the outcome clearly. The worst condition is to have some people thinking that we are bidding and some thinking we have declined.

Communicate the commitment of resources that was made and the level of effort expected. Be clear about which expenses are authorized and who is to participate.

WHAT	WHO
Strategy	Sales Lead
Attend Pre-bid Meeting	Subject Matter Expert
Travel	Engineering Lead
Engage Consultants	Consultants
Prepare Graphics	Graphics Department
Estimate	Estimators
Visit Subcontractors	Contracts Team
Build Price Model	Pricers
Write Content	Technical Writers

Chapter 44 We Won! Transition to Ops

*The first step at which a project is at risk is
the hand-off from the business development team
to the execution and delivery team.*

Transition

In most organizations, the business development team reports to a different chain of command than the delivery team and each is measured by different, often conflicting metrics. The sales team is supposed to maximize revenue, while the delivery team is supposed to maximize profit. Both *should* want to improve reputation, but rarely is that need planned for.

Hand-Over

Hand-Over is the set of important activities that should occur during the transition from sales to ops. All too often there is no formal handover. The checklist below identifies a set of activities the sales team should do to complete the sales cycle, and the related artifacts that should be delivered to the ops team.

Checklist

This checklist is lightweight documentation for a process which belongs to the business development (sales) team, which is agnostic about which operations department handles delivery. At different companies, this is known as Delivery, Deployment, Engineering or Systems Integration Departments.

Even in an environment where the personnel involved in capture will be part of the delivery, this is a good discipline as a precursor to the project kick-off meeting, which is a process owned by the delivery team. In a well-run business unit, although some sales people attend the project kick-off meeting, most of the questions asked during the project kick-off should *already* have been answered by the sales team in the transition meeting and in the transition folder files.

No	Done	Task Description
1		Update the CRM/ sales tracking record with contract amount and revenue dates
2		Create internal stakeholders list to invite to transition meeting
3		Create folder named "Transition" to put required files in
4		Place the following file types in the transition folder with usable* names. (* see immersion training for filename guidance)
5		- Signed contract
6		- RFP and all supplemental client procurement documents
7		- Final technical proposal
8		- Final customer price proposal
9		- Requirements matrix (internal & external)
10		- Post-proposal client questions & answers documents
11		- Correspondence impacting price, scope, and schedule
12		- Oral presentation PowerPoint and handouts
13		- Final price model with all BAFO and negotiation adjustments
14		- Vendor quotes (and any subcontract documents)
15		- Sales tax exemption certificate
16		- Performance bond
17		- Insurance certificates
18		- Client/consultant/subcontractor contact list
19		Create PowerPoint with:
20		- Slide 1: Client Name, project name, client PM, our PM, NTP date, Acceptance Date
21		- Slide 2: Client and consultant names, roles, priorities, personalities
22		- Slide 3: Price breakdown - Subcontractors, equipment, labor, license fees, target profit
23		- Slide 4: Scope – Limited to risks to mitigate, not ordinary work
24		- Slide 5: Schedule highlights – Award, execution, NTP, Design, Development, FAT, First Article, Installation, Acceptance.
25		Schedule a transition meeting to provide the project team with working knowledge of price, scope and schedule commitments to optimize on-time, on-budget, on-scope performance with maximum margin
26		Conduct hand-off meeting with the Deployment Team. Present PowerPoint. Answer questions. PM to document all start-up action items by capturing description, assignee, and due date. Issue at top of meeting notes. Follow-up action items daily.
27		Capture any Sales Rep action items required for closeout and add them to this checklist (not PM's list)
28		Complete the Sales Rep closeout action items
29		Closeout the booking in CRM.
30		This completes transition. Start follow-on business development process.

Part 8 – Career

An organization filled with honest, motivated, connected,
eager, learning, experimenting, ethical and driven people
will always defeat the one that merely has talent.
*– **Every time.***

~ Seth Godin, *September 18, 2013*

Chapter 45 Four Hiring Principles

First who, then what. It matters who you have on the bus.

~ Jim Collins, *Good to Great*

Not So

I started hiring people when I was in college. Back then, I assumed everyone had the same work ethic that I did and that skill was all that you needed in a candidate. *Not so.*

It turns out that there are people who only want a paycheck and are willing to do as little as they can to collect it. I understood this theoretically, but it took a while to truly understand that there really were people who prefer to put substantial effort into *not* working. When you go to hire, you need to look for four separate characteristics:

1. Skill

People need to have the right skills to do the work. This is the obvious one that I thought was sufficient.

2. Drive

Employees need to want to do the work. If they are not self-motivated to do good work, you can't make them. Early on, I assumed everyone wanted to work hard like me. When I was a young engineer at the US DOT Transportation Systems Center, one of the techs who had been working at that building since the days when it was NASA actually told me to slow down otherwise our boss would expect us to work fast all the time. He was talking about my walking pace in the hallways.

3. Culture Fit

This also surprised me. Not everyone can adapt to culture, so you have to look for people who will fit in and get along with their work peers. Otherwise, no one likes them or likes to work with them, and their ideas and requests are all handled inefficiently.

4. Mental Health

Only recently have I realized the need to look for mental health in a candidate. People can have the right skills, want to work, fit the culture, but have some mental issue that periodically erupts, rendering them a liability. I'm not talking about being a little quirky. I mean unstable enough that people start to filter their comments and reactions out of fear of a big work interruption. This slows down communication, lowers trust, and dilutes a positive work environment.

Trust is a key element here. You need to be able to trust an employee enough to be able to speak frankly and honestly with them and not be parsing your own words for fear of setting them off.

All economic activity...requires products of <u>nature</u>; <u>human resources</u>; and <u>capital</u>... The business must be able to attract all three and to put them to productive use. A business that cannot attract the people and the capital it needs will not last long. – Peter Drucker

The original hiring rule for Fog Creek Software, stolen from Microsoft, was *Smart, and Gets Things Done.* Even before they started the company, they realized that they should add a third rule: *Not a jerk.*

It can be really hard to figure all of this out when interviewing a job candidate, and sometimes you hire someone and they just don't work out, which brings us to firing.

Chapter 46 Good Firing

You have to get the wrong people off of the bus.

~ Jim Collins, *Good to Great (2001)*

As soon as you become a manager of people, instead of just things, you are accountable to your organization to be a steward of people's time and the money it costs to employ them. One of the most important lessons I learned in this area was that **firing is even more important than hiring.**

If you leave a misfit employee in place, it impacts everyone who has to work with them. It causes people to question *your* judgment and to get discouraged about "who's on the bus".

As soon as you know that an employee is not going to work out, take action. Waiting just makes it harder.

If an employee consumes more of their peers' time than they should, or if their errors create more work than they produce, they are a net drain on the organization, producing negative value.

Similarly, if someone is good at their job technically, but is poisoning the workplace with a negative, critical, unhelpful, or discouraging attitude, even if their own output is good, by impacting the productivity of others, they may be costing more than they produce.

Firing people is really tough work. In business, there is nothing worse to have to do, but you **must in order to act for the greater good**.

You are not doing a misfit employee any favors by keeping them in a position they are not good at. In fact, you are robbing them of time they could be doing something they can be good at, and thrive in.

Far too frequently, spineless managers transfer and promote people away from their departments, passing off the problem to another part of the company. Eventually, the employee comes to rest in a position where they slowly drain energy and productivity from those around them.

Chapter 47 Finding a Job

*Choose a job you love, and you will never have
to work a day in your life.*

~ Confucius

Hard to, right?

Instead of looking for an employer who can do something for you, look for a company where you can provide great value.

Don't even consider taking a job you are not qualified* for, unless that is part of the explicit agreement. Don't take a job you can't do, and don't take a job under false pretenses.

Rites of Passage, by John Lucht, is my favorite book about changing jobs. It is a very revealing exposé on how professional recruiters work and what goes on in the hiring process. It is full of unconventional advice about getting a good deal when landing a job.

It was lent to me by a former client, Will Wolf, when I had lost my job at PSC. He was practicing the smartest job hunting skill there is – helping other people find jobs.

In life and business you reap what you sow. This is inescapable. Go out of your way now to help steer people to jobs and to steer paying work toward colleagues. Return recruiters calls and give them a hand. When you hear of someone looking for work, ask for a copy of their resume and give them any advice you have. It means a lot to know people are in your corner and you never know who knows who.

Don't worry if you are unsure if a job opportunity is a perfect match for a friend or colleague. That is for them and the hiring manager to figure out. Part of your objective is to develop a reputation for being willing to help, so do it liberally. The same is true of RFPs and bids. If you see a piece of work that a colleague might be interested in, hurry and be the first one to bring it to their attention. They will remember you doing this.

---

* Being qualified for the job is different than meeting every attribute in a job posting. Job postings are idealistic, optimistic, overly specific descriptions that do not reflect the actual qualifications needed.

HR is not a Goalie

So many jobs are found through non-traditional methods now. Remember, the need for a new employee develops long before people go to the hassle and trouble of running an ad. Recruiting is a chore. A good résumé is a relief to a hiring manager in need. Send yours in. If you see a job posting that is not for a position you would want, but it tells you that they do your kind of work, send your resume in. You never know when someone is about to leave or be promoted.

And remember that HR is not a goalie. They are a looking to make a hire. They get no credit for how many applications they weed out. Recruiting is a match-making process. Be helpful now. Ease someone's pain. Help them give you a good job.

Sow Seed Now

Hopefully, you have been proactive about your career. Making connections with people by helping them as you go along in your career is the smartest thing you can do. Make friends before you need them. Whether you are out of work now or not, start helping people.

> Go out of your way to help connect people to jobs
> and to steer paying work toward colleagues - now.

Chapter 48 Getting Fired

Getting fired is really hard work.

What Went Wrong?

Let's assume that you weren't trying to get fired and that you did not get caught doing something illegal. In fact, let's assume that you thought you were doing okay.

Suddenly, you have a short-notice meeting (maybe zero notice) with your manager or HR and they tell you your services are no longer required. The next few minutes are likely to be a dazed blur as they explain what your severance terms are and about COBRA benefits and unemployment etc.

If you are lucky, you make it out the door without falling apart.

What?

You call someone sympathetic and they say, "WHAT? Why did they fire you?" And that's when you realize, you really don't know why.

Maybe they gave you an official reason. Maybe they talked about cutting costs, off-shoring, declining sales or maybe they are tight-lipped since that is the safest bet to avoid problems.

But for the next hours and days, you will wonder, "Why me? Why now?" and then you will start developing theories about what the real story is. You will re-interpret the events of the past year and start to wonder if they had something to do with it. Were there signs you missed? (Yes, there were and you did miss them.)

Should you have worked harder? Been nicer? Spoken up more? Kept your mouth shut more? Not made a joke? Not voiced a criticism? Did pushing for your last pay raise cause this? Did someone tell a lie about you? And it goes on and on.

I Hate Them All

This is a very common reaction. Shed it as soon as you can. It does you no good. Don't tell a lot of people your negative thoughts. It makes you unpleasant to be around.

Instead, talk about everything that you learned at your last job.

It is really easy to let conversations about your firing play in your head. Don't give these thoughts traction in your mental soundtrack.

Instead, run through the answers you will give to tough questions at your next job interview. Dwell on your qualifications.

Want to be really set free? Pray for the prosperity of those who wronged you. See R.T. Kendall's book "Total Forgiveness" for a wonderful treatise on this topic.

Chapter 49 Titles and Cards

What's in a name? That which we call a rose by any other name would smell as sweet.

~ William Shakespeare

What Is a Title Used For?

When it comes to your title, you have to put yourself in the shoes of the people who are hearing/seeing it:

- To your customer, it is an assurance that they are speaking with the right person; that they are being given the attention they deserve.

- Within your industry, it is a standard for comparison; it is the easiest path people have for assessing your level of skill and competency.

- It can mean everything or nothing to your co-workers depending on the size of the company.

- With your potential customers, it can be used as a selling point to gain trust and grow confidence.

- A potential employer or headhunter may use it as a filter, for better or worse.

Elevator Pitch for Your Title

Unfortunately, many people won't be given the opportunity to choose or modify their official title. It is still useful to evaluate your title. It can help you prepare for interactions with these people; you may even realize that you need an elevator speech for explaining your job (which you should have anyway). If your official title is clumsy, don't feel compelled to use it. Don't bring it up. State your role instead.

If you are lucky enough to choose your title, take a minute to search for positions with similar titles on LinkedIn; do their responsibilities roughly line up with yours? Play around with keywords and see if there are options that you may not have thought of. Your title will hopefully optimize the viewpoints above but your opinion of it ultimately trumps these. Keep it short, keep it meaningful and get your elevator speech ready.

Business Card is a Marketing Document

Remember that a business card is a persuasion tool, not an HR document. Just because your official title in your company's HR system is Associate Specialist III does not mean you have to put it on your business card. That title means nothing to an outsider. Pick a customer facing title that helps people understand who you are. You can pick a title that helps you get your job done better. If your company's process can't print the card correctly, go to a print shop and get the right cards made.

Who Needs a Business Card?

Everyone in your company should have a business card. It is a nice way to make employees feel good. It makes the whole company look more professional. And it is very affordable.

What to Put On a Business Card

If you have four phone numbers, do you want people to use them all? Do you need a fax number? If the best way to contact you is by Skype, why not put that on the card?

You should only put information on the card that is helpful. If you are out of the office frequently, use your mobile phone number. Give serious consideration to using just one phone number that works all the time. Put yourself in the user's position and think about what will help them.

More Than One

There is nothing disingenuous about having more than one business card. When I travel in the Middle East, I use a card printed in Arabic on one side. It has a local office address and my Middle East phone number on it. It also lists my university degree because that is normal there for providing helpful context.

And that is the point of a title and a business card, to provide helpful context. Bend the rules to achieve this.

Part 9 – Original Thoughts

Free advice, worth every penny.

Chapter 50 My Own Inventions

If you know the right thing to do, do it now.

In the introduction I said I wish to take very little credit for these contents, except for a few items, two of which my children will immediately recognize:

"I can't fix it if I don't know it's broken."

"Force is rarely the answer."

As I wrote this, I realized there really were more than two. Here they are.

Can't Fix It If I Don't Know It's Broken

These two practical sayings were created around ordinary household repairs of appliances and lights and cars. I am a handyman and an incorrigible tinkerer and I am always delighted to try and fix something.

I hated to see one of my children suffering with a broken item needlessly. It would cause me angst. I often wanted to open up a shop to repair children's toys that just needed a little bit of technical skill that was beyond their parents' ability. When I was 14, my four year old cousin told my Aunt that, "Charlie can fix anything." He brought me a toy action figure whose head and limbs had fallen off. After a little rubber band surgery, the legend was confirmed.

So I hated to see two things: Living with a problem and forcing something that was clearly in need of repair.

As I write this, I just realized that each of these can have a hidden double-meaning.

"I can't fix it if I don't know it's broken," speaks about our inner selves, too. What do you do that unintentionally hurts people? Would you change if you knew? You have zero chance of changing if you don't know. Study yourself. Get to know how you come across to people. We are all imperfect people and sometimes we are broken in ways that we don't even know.

A great book along these lines is Marshall Goldsmith's, *What Got You Here, Won't Get You There (2007)*.

Force Is Rarely the Answer

You can get your way with force. But if you damage a relationship along the way, is it worth it? This is the logic behind Stephen Covey's *Think Win-Win* idea. Either patience or finesse is usually a better answer. Force is for immediate gratification. Patience is what love produces. Finesse is what skill brings.

Of course, my kids loved it when they brought a problem to me and I said, "Well, force is rarely the answer, but sometimes it is," and then grabbed a hammer and fixed it with a well-placed whack!

The Charlie Test

When doing requirements analysis with my software product development team at PSC in the early 1990s to define a project scope of work, I developed what became called the Charlie test. When the team was done stating the functional requirements, I would ask, "If it does all of these things, but only these things and nothing more, will we have absolutely everything we need?" Invariably, the answer the first time around was, "Well, no…to work, it will need an X."

This method applies equally well to a packing list for a trip, demo, or installation. "If the things on this list are all we have with us, will we be successful?" Often the result of this process was that we identified assumptions about what should be provided by others (e.g., power, Internet, video projector) and then we could create that list and send it ahead for others to verify.

Repository Theory

If you create an organized, well-known set of containers for information, you greatly increase the probability that people will put information in the right place when it comes into their possession. They will also be able to find it and re-use it. It is estimated that over 10% of all the information that a company needs to run its business is re-created from scratch *every year* because it cannot be readily found. Information is a valuable business asset. (See Mike Song's COTA filing system.)

PUTP

Anyone who ever worked on a project where I was project manager learned the constant refrain of "pick up the phone." Technologists are especially prone to doing *anything* other than asking the person who knows the answer. I think it stems from a very well-meaning desire not to disturb other knowledgeable workers when they might be "in the zone" and working productively.

Communication Model

I created this communication model to help people understand software programmer interruption and isolation levels, both of which are needed at various times for productivity.

Interruption and Isolation Levels:

- Conversation (constant, maximum distraction)
- Pairs programming
- Working side by side
- Tap on the shoulder
- Instant messaging
- Email
- Daily stand-up meeting
- Random hallway meeting
- Wait for weekly meeting
- Wait for next unscheduled meeting (minimum distraction)

Subordinate Self Governance

It is each manager's responsibility to teach the people on their team the limits for what they can and cannot decide for themselves and to maximize it.

If I have to wait for a department manager to talk to every time I want to request services from that department, that is a source of delay a business cannot afford. Don't yell at me because one of your department members did something to help me when asked. Instead, teach them what are the normal bounds of activities that anyone can ask them to do and what things they cannot do without getting their department manager's permission. If you need a ticket or charge number, that's fine.

It is not an acceptable answer to say that they have to ask permission before ever helping anyone. This is the practice of petty managers who are afraid to delegate. That approach is too inefficient.

Lowest Cost Resource

Every task at a company should be performed by the least expensive person capable of doing it well. This seems obvious (see chapter 2), but it is amazing how frequently it is ignored. Have you ever created a fax cover sheet? (Maybe you are too young to know what a fax is.) Who books travel at your company, each traveler? Is that a good use of their time? Who enters travel receipts into an expense report? Who sets up video conferences? Maybe these are not the errors your company makes, but you can probably identify some.

Years ago, one of the smartest things B&K did, was to hire a chef and provide a subsidized lunch. This was at a company of less than 75 people, an unheard of number for an in-house chef.

This way, instead of people heading out for hour long lunches, everyone stayed in the building, ate in the cafeteria and frequently transacted business. Lunch was much shorter and more productive. Whatever was spent on a part-time chef and subsidized food was more than made up in time and productive conversation. Plus, the small cafeteria with just two long tables constantly brought people from different departments together.

1000 Efficiencies

Everyone is familiar with the expression "dying a death by 1000 cuts." Most companies that fail (most do), do so because of a large number of small problems, not one large problem (Although you can often trace most of the small problems back to the head of the company).

So how does a company succeed in the long term? Is it the result of a single big stroke of luck? No, it is generally the cumulative effect of doing a large number of small things right. In fact, it is the result of doing a *huge* number of things right. So examine every action, every step, and every facet of every customer interaction looking for a way to improve. It is the sum of 1000 efficiencies that make a company profitable.

1000 Advantages Corollary

Look for a 1000 ways to be better than your competitors. When I managed a national sales force, I conducted a training session where I declared that, yes, we literally want to do everything better than our competitors. We want to return calls more quickly, have clearer email subject lines, and nicer looking price quotes. These are not things that cost a lot of money. They mostly take awareness. No single thing done better will make a company a winner, but if at every turn you are slightly better than your competitors, it won't matter which thing is important to your customer, they will prefer you. Your employees will prefer to work for you too.

Zero Enemies

The correct number of enemies to have in business is zero. People never forget being mistreated. The odds of running into someone again in a professional setting are very high. You can't afford to have people out in the marketplace bad-mouthing you.

Not only is the correct number of enemies to have in business zero, but you can never tell if someone really likes you or is just being polite. Treat people nicely. Help when it is in your power to do so. Sow good seed; it comes back to you.

$10,000 for an Extra Day

At the end of a project, as the go-live date approaches, we would gladly pay $10,000 for an extra day. Those days are free at the beginning of a project.

Year after year, on project after project, I see project teams dawdling at the start of a project as though it is a surprise that they have won the business and signed the contract.

Start doing as much as you can, as early as you can.

Business Velocity

This is an undervalued business concept. In a way, it is related to Goldratt's Theory of Constraints and the effects of chaos. Imagine you are going to drive to meet someone at noon, but you leave 30 seconds late and get caught behind a school bus. The bus won't make a right-on-red turn at the next light, so you wait. As a result, when you get to the railroad crossing, the gate arms are coming down. A small delay has turned into a large one.

This can happen in business too. If you reply to an email a little late, the recipient might miss it because they are starting a meeting. As a result, they don't respond until after the meeting. The response shows up in the inbox of someone who just left for the day. Tomorrow that person forwards it to the person who needs to act on it, but they just left for a week's vacation. If only you had replied faster.

This concept has countless applications in business. An invoice sent out a day early can beat out the arrival and approval of someone else's invoice to a cash strapped company. A tool returned promptly after use to a tool crib can eliminate the need to buy a duplicate tool. An estimate submitted early enables a reviewer to catch an error. A proposal completed early can be sent via a low cost courier rather than via an expensive hand delivery. A resume read early leads to hiring a good candidate who was about to take another job.

Every asset a company has can be used multiple times in a year, and the more turns per year that a fixed cost asset yields, the more productive the dollars used to buy it are. This is well understood in retail, where inventory turns per year are a measure of the effective use of capital, but any asset which costs money can be measured this way.

> Speed is the great multiplier in business

Graphics

In a good graphic, shape, color, proximity, and connecting lines should all have meaning. Have a reason (Other than "That's the order I drew them in") for where things are placed on a diagram. Don't imply sequentiality when none exists.

Tipping

Don't tip based on the service that you got this time, tip based on the service you want next time. Never assume that you will not return to any service provider. It may happen faster than you think. I left a Dim Sum restaurant in San Diego once and a waiter came running out to the parking lot with a small notebook I had left behind on the table. Imagine what would have happened if I had tipped poorly.

When expensing meals and tips to your company or client, round up for the tip to the waiter, and round down on the copy you submit. This makes you look good to both for a very small price out of your pocket.

Three Rules of Gossip

First, if you have something bad to say about someone, say it directly to them before you discuss it with anyone else.

Second, if you have something good to say about someone, say it in front of everyone.

Third, don't gossip.

Chapter 51 Systems Integration Business Model

Many entrepreneurs fail to think of their businesses as
systems, even if their products are complex systems.

The systems integration business can be diagrammed to show the influences of different parts of the business on each other. With the right inputs, you can have agility and productive, happy employees which create the cycle of success.

Most new businesses start out with good employees who are empowered and understand the goals, but somewhere on the road to success, businesses get in a hurry to hire more people and they lower the bar and hire mediocre employees.

The mediocre employees need more guidance and processes. Guidance turns into management, and management turns into supervision. To ease the workload of supervision, processes become rules. Then the focus shifts from doing the right thing to following the rules.

To avoid this, management needs to create feedback loops which promote beneficial behavior. This requires the discipline to hire only good people, which is hard work. It also requires the bravery to be transparent about finances so employees can understand the effects of their decisions.

Management has to do well in these five areas:

- Empowerment
- Risk Tolerance
- Clear Goals
- Transparency and Integrity
- Smart Hiring

These will result in happy employees, profit, and satisfied customers as shown on the diagram on the next page. If you can pull all of these off, you create feedback loops that strengthen your competitiveness and you can dominate your industry.

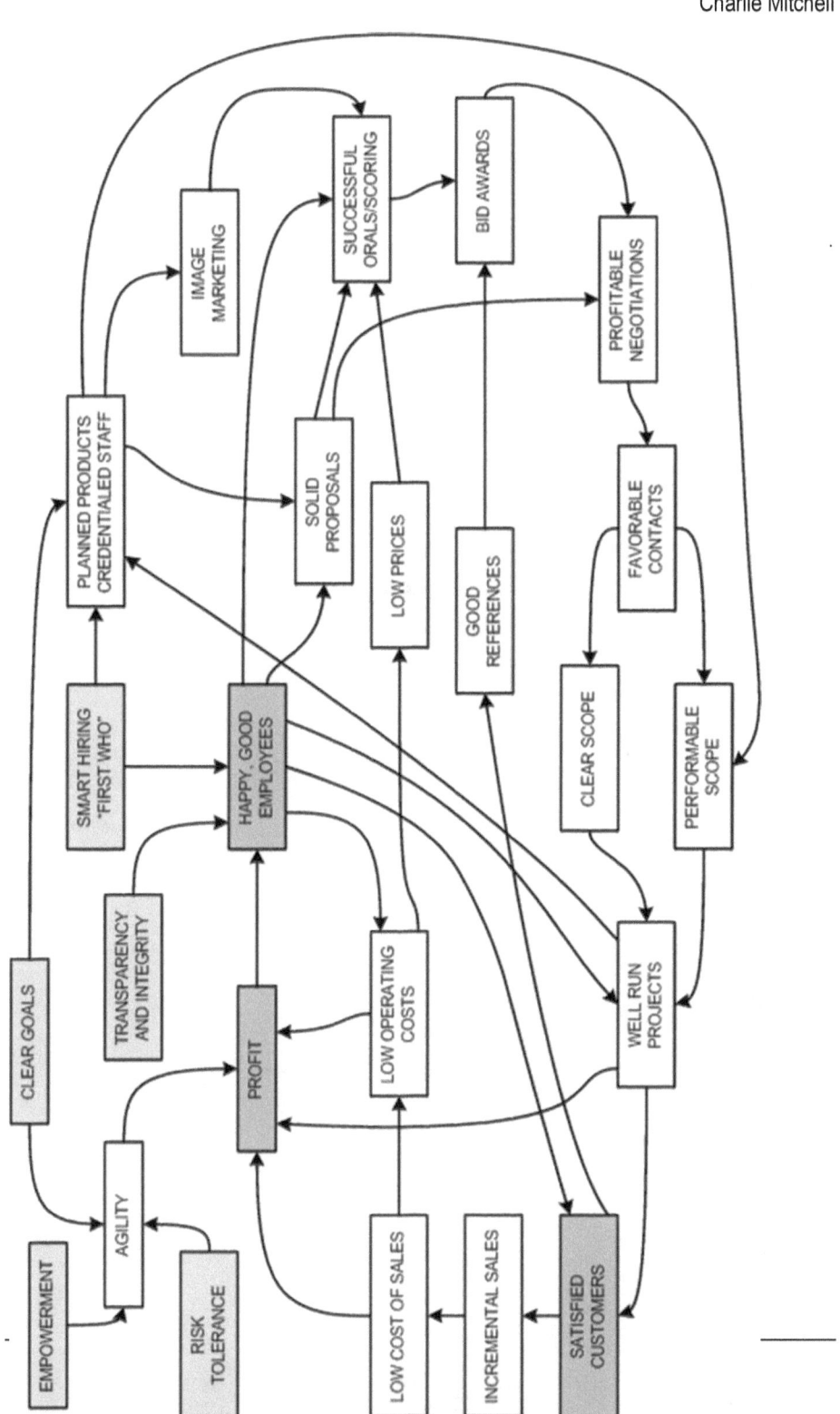

Part 10 – Appendices

But, wait! There's more!

Appendix 1 Charlie's Notes on Business Jargon

Even when people are attempting to speak plainly, they can be hard to understand.

Code

Most of the time, speakers of business lingo are just being lazy, resorting to vague terms. Good or bad, you need to know this lingo to succeed at work.

Decoding

It used to be that if you did not know what a term means, you had to ask and reveal your ignorance. Today, you can Google it. If you don't make the effort to Google it, you may get an irritated response.

If you don't know the terms your company uses, you will appear as an outsider. If you attempt to use them incorrectly or out of keeping with your status in the organization, you will look like a poser. Many business terms have sports origins (home run) or military origins (G2). To wield terms correctly marks you as an insider with management potential. It is a tricky business.

The next part of this book is a business lingo glossary with terms, acronyms and phrases you should know. Some of these will seem very obvious to you because you've known them and used them, but remember they are completely foreign to other people. Others will seem so pretentious or arbitrary that they seem fictional, but they are all in use somewhere.

Appendix 2 Business Jargon

A glossary for new graduates and others wondering what the heck the other cube dwellers mean

Above my pay grade *adj. (phrase)* Refers to information and strategy available only to more senior staff. Military origin.

Above the line *adj.* Financial: value before deducting general and administrative business costs. Advertising: Marketing efforts to unspecified masses.

Action item *n.* Assignment. An appointed task, usually resulting from a meeting. At a well-run company, these are carefully documented, clearly communicated, and systematically followed-up on to ensure timely completion.

Amortize v. Strictly, this is the retirement of debt by paying it over time. This notion of spreading a payment over time has come to incorrectly mean spreading money over multiple categories. Use apportion for this usage.

Annual leave *n.* Government term for vacation. Also known as PTO or Paid Time Off. In Europe, holiday.

AOB *n.* Any other business. For a meeting agenda.

ASAP *adv.* As Soon As Possible. Similar is the less demanding ASAC or As Soon As Convenient.

Availability *n.* Unallocated time open for an assignment. Distinct from capability or skill to do an assignment.

BAFO *n.* Best And Final Offer. In procurement, a resubmission of price and terms as a final stage of bidding for work.

Ballpark *v.* Estimate. Guess. Spitball. Throw darts. See SWAG: Scientific Wild-Assed-Guess.

Bandwidth *n.* Capacity to do work. Borrowed from electronic information transmission.

Beneficial use *n.* The occupancy or successful utilization of the project work pending final, formal approval or acceptance. Often this triggers the start of warranty, maintenance, or a milestone payment. May correspond with substantial completion.

Bid/No-bid decision *n.* In business development and sales, the formal process of deciding whether or not to invest the time and cost of pursuing a piece of work. Decisions are based on factors such as probability of winning, anticipated profit, effect on company image, availability of staff and capital, cash flow, technical and schedule risk, impact on other projects, and ongoing operations.

Bonding *v.* To provide a financial guarantee that you will perform the work promised. Bonds (e.g., bid bond, performance bond, and payment bond) are bought for approximately one percent of the price of the project (per year) from large financial surety companies. In the event of breach of contract, the bond is pulled. The bonding company will then come after you for damages.

Brief *v.* To provide summary information about recent events, often in preparation for a meeting, or right after one (the latter is better known as debrief).

BPO *n.* Business process outsourcing. Hiring another company to do non-core business for you.

Brown field *n.* A project site which has previously been built on. Contrast with *green field*.

Budget *n.* The amount of money planned, requested, and authorized to spend on operating costs or resources.

Burn rate *n.* Rate of expenditure of cash on a project or especially at a start-up business.

Business development *v.* Synonymous with sales. Also, the strategic acquisition of other companies. As a noun, it sometimes refers to the sales team within an organization.

Business plan *n.* A document describing a business's strategy for issues such as product, staff, finance, geography, competitors, and customers.

Business Velocity *n.* The rate of conducting business which has a huge impact of the use of capital and resources. The accumulation of many small timing advances or delays.

Buy-in *n.* Agreement and support of an idea.

Capability maturity model *n.* A hierarchical ranking of software development organizations' level of ability to consistently create good software ranked into five levels. From the Carnegie Mellon Software Engineering Institute. Versions have been adapted for other fields of work, like engineering.

Cap-X *n.* Capital expenditure. A measure of the use of the company's market capitalization money. Also CapEx.

C-Level *adj.* Reference to various chief officers of a company. CXO means chief blank(X) officer where the blank, or X, is executive, finance, information, marketing, technology, strategy and other less frequent roles. Also, collectively C-suite.

COB *n.* Close of business. As in, *Your report is due by COB Tuesday.*

COGS *n.* Cost Of Goods Sold. A major expense on a company's income statement that drives profitability.

Circle back *v.* Revisit an issue. As in, *Put that idea in the parking lot and we'll circle back to it later.*

Commander's Intent *n.* A clear and concise expression of the purpose of the operation and the desired military end state that supports mission command, provides focus to the staff, and helps subordinate and supporting commanders act to achieve the commander's desired results without further orders, even when the operation does not unfold as planned.

Contingency *n.* The buffer, margin, padding, or cushion added to a budget or estimate to account for unforeseen difficulties or delays.

Critical path *n.* The sequence of tasks with zero slack between them which constrain the minimum project duration.

Cube *n.* Short for cubicle; the door-less workspace created by three short movable walls. Usually created in clusters of multiple cubes. As in, *Leave the left-over meeting food for the cube dwellers to eat.*

Cycle time *n.* The time it takes for a process to run from beginning to the next beginning.

Deck *n.* Slide presentation using PowerPoint or Keynote. At one time it referred to a stack of charts, projector transparencies or *foils.*

Delta *n.* Change or difference, as in the delta between two numbers.

DMAIC *n.* From Lean Six Sigma: Define, measure, analyze, improve, control.

Dog and pony show *n.* Presentation or demonstration. Usually more involved than just a slide presentation. May include hardware or software demonstrations.

Domain Expertise *n.* Knowledge about a particular subject matter.

Drive *v.* To push forward with an idea or approach, or to advocate for a position or the use of a specific resource (e.g., drive growth).

Due diligence *n.* Fact finding research, especially for company merger and acquisition work.

EOM *n.* End Of Message. Used at the end of an email subject line where the subject line is the entire message.

EBIT/EBITDA *n.* Earnings Before Interest Taxes/Earnings Before Interest Taxes Depreciation Amortization. A measure of how much cash a business generates from operations.

Feature thinning *v.* Elimination of unnecessary software functions at the beginning of a software development project. Contrast with *scope creep*.

FY *n.* Fiscal Year. Financial Year. Not all companies run their accounting year January to December.

Fly-off *n.* Direct competition between short-listed firms, usually involving a prototype or pilot test. Also known as a "Bake off"

First pass *n.* An initial draft or first draft of a document, recognizing that multiple revisions are required to make a good document an excellent document.

FUD *n.* Fear, Uncertainty, Doubt. Used to steer someone away from a course of action by making it appear risky. A marketing technique used by companies traditionally viewed as *safe* choices.

G2 *n.* Secret or hard to get intelligence; competitive information, including pricing. Derived from the military designation of a General's intelligence staff office.

Gantt chart *n.* In project management, a graphical technique for showing task chronology. Not good at showing dependency. See Project Network.

Gap Analysis v. Figuring out the parts missing from your existing system, team or solution needed for the next project. Common in system integration project and product marketing planning.

Go-live v. Start-up of a system, project, business or other endeavor. As a noun, the date for going on-line or start of revenue service.

Governance n. Formal oversight of an organization's activities, often by a board of senior personnel, designed to ensure compliance with principles, values and laws. Frequently performed via formal reviews resulting in official approvals.

Green field n. A fresh start, especially for a new building or research project. Contrast with brown field.

Hard stop n. Immovable time commitment. As in, *I have a hard stop at 11:00, so let's pick up the pace.*

HR n. Human Resources department. Responsible for hiring, firing, benefits administration, and sometimes payroll.

Hyper-productivity n. A state of very productive work due to clear focus.

Intelligence v. Sensitive business information about the actions of other parties which provides some advantage. Often abbreviated to just "intel." Military origin.

Interface v. Interact with. Talk to. Correspond with.

IVR n. Interactive Voice Response. Automatic computerized phone system with spoken prompts for caller choices.

Knowledge base n. A collection of useful, reusable business information.

KPIs n. Key Performance Indicators. Metrics selected to measure and evaluate because they are important signs of conditions.

Lean *adj.* Work done in a way that eliminates the eight wastes which are: excess motion, transportation, defects/scrap/rework, excess production, inventory, waiting, over processing, and non-utilized employee creativity/ideas.

Learning curve *n.* The rate at which a new skill, field, or business area can be understood. Normally viewed as expensive dues to pay to enter a new area of endeavor.

Level-set *v.* Provide information to provide everyone with the same background about a topic, usually at the start of a meeting.

Long pole in the tent *n.* The task in a project with the longest duration, or that controls the end date. Sometimes loosely used to mean the biggest problem in a situation.

Lunch and learn *n.* Lunch time training session. Also called brown-bag symposium.

Market (segment) *n.* A conceptual area to do business in, defined by location, product category, demographic or industry sector.

Marketecture *n.* High level, often undeveloped, conceptual description of a technical solution. More likely a fanciful idea of the marketing department than an actual product plan that engineering is building. See *slideware* and *vaporware*.

Meeting Notice *n.* An invitation to a meeting sent by email. Predominant among companies using MS-Outlook for email and calendar functions.

Metcalf's Law *n.* The value of a telecommunications network is proportional to the square of the number of connected users of the system (n^2).

Minimum Viable Product *n.* A product with the smallest set of functions needed to make it marketable. Used frequently with software.

Module *n.* A sub-component of a system. Can also apply to a portion of a project or program such as training program module.

Moore's Law *n.* The observation that, over the history of computing hardware, the number of transistors, and therefore computing power, in a dense integrated circuit doubles approximately every two years.

Muda, Mura, Mari *n.* The three wastes of lean manufacturing or lean process: Roughly equal to Waste, Unevenness, Overburden

Negative slack *n.* The difference in time between the short time available and longer time a task will actually take to complete.

Net *n.* Bottom line profit after all expenses.

Net-net *n.* Gist, bottom line concept, end result, at the end of the day. This is very business-speak, so avoid using.

NRN – No Reply Needed. Often in an email subject line.

Off-line *n.* Later, after this meeting, with a smaller group of participants. Often used to duck accountability for an awkward subject, as in *Let's take this topic off-line.*

One throat to choke *n.* One person to hold responsible. Also, one belly-button to poke.

Open kimono *n.* Politically (gender) incorrect term from the 1980s for full disclosure or transparency.

OPM *n.* Other People's Money.

Padding *n.* Cushion, contingency, or buffer added to a selling price or a time estimate to account for risk.

Paradigm shift *n.* Big change in thinking and perspective, often based on changing methods or priorities. Has become business speak, but they do happen and are needed for major improvements.

Parking lot *n.* A written list of ideas to be discussed in the future. Often on a large pad of paper on an easel in the corner. Used to keep meetings from drifting off topic.

Pilot *n.* An initial test run or trial.

Ping *v.* Make an inquiry of someone for a simple answer or to remind.

Pitch *v.* Present an idea. As a noun, presentation. See *deck*. Borrowed from baseball.

POC *n.* Point Of Contact. As in, *We need one person to act as the single point of contact for contract changes.* Also, *Proof of Concept.*

Poka-Yoke *n.* In lean manufacturing, a mechanism that prevents an operator from being able to make a mistake, thereby avoiding creating waste. Generally, any deliberate safeguard to make people succeed.

Project *n.* According to the Project Management Institute, a project is a temporary group activity designed to produce a unique product, service or result.

Project network view *n.* Graphical technique for showing dependency, not good for showing time. See *Gantt chart*.

PTO *n.* Paid Time Off, meaning vacation time in the USA. (In farm equipment, power take-off.)

Punch List *n.* A list of workmanship or deliverable deficiencies at the end of a project which must be resolved before final acceptance and payment is granted. Occurs after *substantial completion* and often after the owner has taken over the site.

Push back *v.* Question, resist, or argue against.

P-Win *n.* Probability of winning a proposal or bid.

Quick win *n*. To obtain an early successful outcome from an effort to improve morale, support, or perception.

Quality *n*. Conformance with customer requirements.

Ramp up *v*. Slowly increase, as in capacity or output.

Reach out *v*. Inquire, ask, probe; especially for uncommon information.

Real-time *adv*. As it happens; live. Borrowed from computer science.

RIF *n*. Reduction In Force. Euphemism for layoffs, like downsizing, surplusing, terminating, or right-sizing.

Red team review *n*. Almost final review of a complete document or proposal before it goes to senior management for gold team review.

Red flag *n*. A warning or indicator that there is a problem or risk which must be addressed before proceeding. Failure to recognize a red flag that could have prevented a current problem is a bad failure.

Re-mission *v*. To re-purpose and reuse some idea, design, resource or asset.

Report *n*. A direct report is a manager's immediate subordinate.

Reserve *n*. Contingency or padding. Capacity to deal with unanticipated costs or delays.

Resource *n*. In project management; the manpower, facilities, materials and machines required to perform a task.

Retainage *n*. A portion of a project's progress payment withheld as leverage to ensure project completion. Retainage ranges from five to ten percent. Retainage is released after the punch list is completed (see *substantial completion*). Next, the system is formally accepted and final payment is made.

RFP/RFQ *n.* In procurement, a Request for Proposal or Request for Quote. In RFPs, companies propose similar functional solutions. In RFQs, companies propose identical scope and terms and only price matters. Less commonly, Request for Bid. Don't make the mistake of calling your proposal an RFP.

RFI *n.* Request for information to help a customer write an RFP.

Road Show *n.* In venture capital, taking a start-up company's business proposition around to potential investors.

Runway *n.* The amount of time or budget available to complete a task. As in, *We don't have enough runway to get this on-line before Christmas.*

Sales *v.* Synonymous with *business development.* As a noun, it refers to the sales team or department within an organization.

Seat on the bus *n.* Position and role within an organization. *Get the right people on the bus, the wrong people off the bus, and everyone in the right seat on the bus.* – Jim Collins, *Good to Great (2001).*

Scope creep *n.* Increase in project scope beyond the amount contracted for. Contrast with *feature thinning.*

Silo *n.* An isolated department or functional area within a company. Typically has the negative connotation that one silo does not communicate or *play well* with another silo.

Six Sigma *n.* A data driven quality improvement approach which uses the DMAIC method: Define, Measure, Analyze, Improve, and Control.

Shoot the messenger *v.* To be angry with the person delivering bad news. This is a sure way to stop the flow of information from the front line to senior management. Can be as subtle as disagreeing with the magnitude of the problem. Embracing bad news is the smart move.

Short list *n.* The list of companies bidding on a project who make the cut and are asked to take the next step in the process, such as making an oral presentation of their proposed solution.

Slideware *n.* Software which exists only in the mind of the presenter. See *vaporware*.

Slack *n.* In project management, the difference in time between how long a task takes and the time available when the time is positive. See *negative slack*.

SMART goal *n.* A well-defined goal clarified with five criteria: Specific, measurable, attainable, relevant, and time based.

SME *n.* Subject Matter Expert. Someone with strong knowledge of a specific topic.

Socialize *v.* Circulate an idea to gain support and approval.

Soft pedal *v.* Gently push forward an idea, while understating the severity. Often involves telling an incomplete story.

Solution *n.* In procurement, the sum total of scope, approach, price, schedule, financial resources, staff, technology, team partners, suppliers, design, quality, installation, training, warranty, maintenance, technical support, service, and operations that comprise the offer. Incorrectly used as a verb with increasing frequency.

Stick to the knitting *v. phrase* Focus on what you are proven to be good at doing. Don't diversify too much. From Tom Peters', *In Search of Excellence*.

Straw-man *n.* Mock-up or outline of a design, concept, proposal or plan for early review purposes. As a verb, to create a mock-up or outline of a design, concept, proposal or plan for early review purposes.

Strategic *adj.* Long term, large scope, conceptual. Compare to tactical. A strategy can be comprised of a set of tactics.

Stretch goal *n.* An additional level of performance beyond what is agreed to as baseline performance.

SWAG *n.* Scientific Wild-Ass Guess. A ballpark estimate or guesstimate.

Substantial completion *n.* In project management or construction, the stage when enough of the work is completed to permit *beneficial use* or occupancy of the project work. Remaining items go on a punch list to be completed.

Swim lane *n.* Process flow diagram which segments responsibility into columns or rows and indicates areas of responsibility.

Table *v.* Start or stop discussing a topic depending on the current condition. Stopping is similar to *take off-line*. Starting is similar to surface or broach, as in, *I'd like to put Q3 sales on the table*.

Tactical *adj.* Near term, small scope, practical. Compare to *strategic*.

Task *n.* In project management, an individual unit of work which can be estimated and assigned.

Tender *n.* Imprecise United Kingdom term for a request for proposal. Also used to mean a bid. As a verb, to release an RFP; also to submit a bid.

That dog won't hunt – That idea does not have merit or make sense. It is implausible.

Throw under the bus *v.* To position someone to be blamed. Often said hypocritically, as in, *I don't want to throw him under the bus, but he was supposed to finish yesterday*.

Tiger team *n.* A short-lived task force assigned to solve a single problem.

TLA *n.* Three letter acronym. Deliberately humorous.

Tollgate *n.* A barrier or threshold in a process. An end-of-stage test in Six-Sigma. A set of criteria when passing from one proposal stage to the next.

Toolkit *n.* A collection of assets, skills, techniques, etc. used to solve a problem.

Transparency *n.* Free disclosure of information, especially financial. Revealing motives or goals. Admitting weaknesses and failures.

Tribal knowledge *n.* Process or client knowledge that is not documented, but exists only as company folklore. Hard to train on this.

Turn-key *adj.* Finished, ready-to-use, all encompassing. Or having all of the components needed in kit form.

Upside *n.* Benefit, positive aspect, redeeming quality. *There is not enough upside to justify the down-side risk.*

Value proposition *n.* Intrinsic worth of a sales or other offer. Also, *value prop.*

Value add *n.* The increase in worth brought by a person, company, or resource investment. As an adjective, *Value-added.*

Vaporware *n.* A product, especially software, which does not yet exist, except as a concept. See *slideware* and *marketecture.*

Visibility *n.* Degree of conspicuousness to senior management. Access to valuable information.

Vision *n.* Bold leadership direction. Part of the Mission, Vision, Values trio. Sometimes confused with principles.

Venture capital *n.* Investment money from commercial sources who lend in exchange for high returns, and managerial control of start-ups or growing companies.

Wheelhouse *n.* Area of strength and expertise. More like *strong suit* than *bailiwick* or *court.*

Win-win deal *n.* A negotiation where both parties are getting a good outcome. Popularized by Stephen Covey, who explained that it is often the result of *seeking first to understand, then be understood* and *synergistic thinking.*

WBS *n.* Work Breakdown Structure. In project management, a detailed list of tasks and subtasks to be estimated, sequenced and scheduled.

Work by others *n.* In contract scope of work language, this term identifies items on a blue print that are part of the project, but are assigned to be performed by another party and consequently do not need to be considered in cost estimating or scheduling.

Yield *n.* The output or outcome of a process. Often measured as a percentage of the output divided by the input.

Zero-sum thinking *n.* A mindset that assumes that in order for one person to get more, someone else must get less. The opposite of abundance thinking. Synergistic thinking assumes that the right answer is to make more pie, not just get a wider slice.

Appendix 3 Book List

This is the list of books which have shaped my thinking over the past 30+ years.

You don't have to like these particular books, but you should be able to answer these questions:

- What is your favorite book on business overall?
- What is your favorite book on leadership and management?
- What is your favorite book on sales and marketing?
- What is your favorite book on hiring and staff development?
- What is your favorite book on efficiency?

My Top Five Choices

It is really hard to pick just five favorite books, but here is my current set, in the order that I read them. If a company practices these teachings, it will dominate its field.

- *The Speed of Trust*; Stephen M. R. Covey *(2008)*
- *The Seven Habits of Highly Effective People*; Stephen R. Covey *(1989)*
- *The Five Dysfunctions of a Team*; Pat Lencioni *(2002)*
- *Good To Great*; Jim Collins *(2001)*
- *The One Minute Manager;* Ken Blanchard *(1982)*

Other Favorites *(alphabetical)*

- *Advantage, The*; Pat Lencioni *(2012)* A top five candidate
- *Back of The Napkin, The*; Dan Roam *(2008)* Communicating with pictures; http://www.thebackofthenapkin.com
- *Beyond Bullet Points*; Cliff Atkinson *(2011)* Slide presentations

- *Critical Chain*; Eliyahu M. Goldratt *(1997)* Goldratt's application of TOC to project work

- *Crossing The Chasm: Marketing and Selling High-Tech Products to Mainstream Customers*; Geoffrey Moore *(2009)*

- *Death By Meeting*; Pat Lencioni *(2004)*

- *Dilbert Principle, The*; Scott Adams *(1997)* OA5

- *Don't Make Me Think*; Steve Krug *(2005)* Software user interface design and low-cost testing

- *E-Myth Manage, The/E-Myth Revisited, The*; Michael Gerber *(2004, 2009)* Document processes via franchising methods

- *Eats, Shoots & Leaves: The Zero Tolerance Approach to Punctuation*; Lynne Truss, *(2003)*

- *Getting Things Done*; David Allen *(2015)* Personal effectiveness

- *Gifted Boss, The*; Dale Dauten *(2011)* Free from management, mediocrity and morons

- *Great By Choice*; Jim Collins *(2011)* A top five candidate

- *Hamster Revolution, The;* Mike Song *(2007)* Efficiency

- *In Search of Excellence*; Tom Peters *(2012)* Eight common traits: Bias toward action, Closeness to customer, Autonomy and Entrepreneurship, Productivity through people, Hands-on value driven, Stick to knitting, Simple form-lean staff, Simultaneous loose-tight properties

- *Linchpin*; Seth Godin *(2010)* Make art, give gifts, become crucial

- *Made to Stick;* Chip and Dan Heath *(2007)* Simple marketing principles for effective messages.

- *Mastering the Rockefeller Principles;* Vern Harnish *(2002)* Simple pragmatic techniques for efficient company management

- *Practice of Management, The*; Peter Drucker *(2010)* Original classic

- *Read This Before Our Next Meeting*; Al Pittampalli *(2011)* Meetings are broken; they should ratify, not make decisions

- *Smart and Gets Things Done*; Avram Joel Spolsky *(2007)* Recruiting; making staff productive

- *Spin Selling*; Neil Rackham *(1988)* Situation, problem, implication, need-payoff

- *Straight From the Gut*; Jack Welch *(2003)* Cull the bottom 10% and the reward top 20% by 200-300% more than average.

- *Swim With The Sharks Without Being Eaten Alive*; Harvey Mackay *(2009)* Always hire good people when you find them

- *Switch*; Chip and Dan Heath *(2010)* Managing change

- *Tribes*; Seth Godin *(2008)* Create an identity group; not for everyone

- *What Got You Here, Won't Get You There;* Marshall Goldsmith *(2007)* Don't overuse strengths as a leader.

- *Who Moved My Cheese*; Spencer Johnson *(1998)* Accepting and working with change productively.

Favorite Management Movie

This movie is said to have been used in more management training sessions than any other movie:

12 O'clock High – Starring Gregory Peck – Severe wartime management doctrine.

www.ingramcontent.com/pod-product-compliance
Lightning Source LLC
Chambersburg PA
CBHW030940180526
45163CB00002B/640

9780359155316